Survival Vocabulary

Gertrude Welder

J. WESTON
WALCH
PUBLISHER
Portland, Maine

Cover photograph © Skjold Photographs

1   2   3   4   5   6   7   8   9   10

ISBN 0-8251-2843-9

Copyright © 1981, 1996
J. Weston Walch, Publisher
P. O. Box 658 • Portland, Maine 04104-0658

Printed in the United States of America

Contents

To the Teacher

Survival Vocabulary is a series of vocabulary exercises for students with special needs. It has been prepared to motivate students to enrich their vocabularies while having fun.

The two hundred words in this ten-unit set are basic functional words that all people living in a community should know. The list does not contain *all* the words necessary for survival in society, but the words that are included would, if learned, make a substantial contribution to a student's daily usable and vital vocabulary.

Since students retain information better when it is presented in categories, the two hundred vocabulary words in this set have been separated by topic into ten units. Each unit has twenty words and contains eleven learning exercises based on these words.

The objective of the set is a simple but well-proven one: to teach students these words by presenting them in eleven different ways in eleven different exercises. Each exercise uses a different approach, and the variety plus the repetition help to teach the words and reinforce the students' new-gained knowledge. Six additional activities can be used with each unit to further reinforce and secure this knowledge. Activities involving the student with a partner provide additional review while increasing motivation and enhancing the student's self-image.

This material is presented in blackline master format so that you may reproduce as many copies as necessary, and so that the student may work on each exercise, using as many sheets as necessary until that exercise is mastered. The student should not be introduced to the following exercise until the preceding one has been mastered. Successive exercises are continued until mastery of the words in that unit is achieved. Individual student needs may dictate which units will be approached initially and in what order the units will be used. The six supplementary activities—also blackline masters—can be reproduced to make enough copies for use with all units and may be used at your discretion.

Each unit of eleven exercises should be made up into an individual workbook or folder for each student. Lower-ability students find a workbook format to be more satisfactory than separate handout sheets, and the blackline master format allows you to use a workbook concept at a fraction of the ready-made workbook cost. Either you or the student can make up the workbook, but it should be put together before the student begins working on any of the exercise sheets.

Encourage your students to design their own original covers for the workbooks, using markers, crayons, pens, or cutouts from sources such as magazines, fliers, catalogs, or paper placemats. Beginning students and slower learners will be motivated by the individualized format of the workbooks. And the booklets will be available for review and display, and for students to share with friends and parents.

We hope you and your students will enjoy working with *Survival Vocabulary* and that these lessons will prove a valuable experience for everyone involved.

Directions for Exercises and Activities

Each unit in this set presents twenty vocabulary words appropriate to the unit's title. The majority of the words are simple, everyday terms that your students regularly hear, say, read, or write. The eleven different learning exercises using these words are repeated in each unit. The six supplementary activities are in a form that can be used with all units. Directions follow to help you effectively use the exercises and activities.

Exercise 1: New Words and Lost Letters

Objectives: • To learn the twenty words and their definitions
  • To learn how to spell the words by filling in the spaces with the missing letters

Twenty vocabulary words are given with very simple definitions. The student sees the visual sequence of each letter in each word when the missing letters are written in the Lost Letters column. The student may look at the word list on the left of the page to ensure correct spelling or may cover the word list and try to recall the correct letter sequence.

Exercise 2: Snoop and Solve

Objective: • To find each of the twenty words in a maze, circle the word, and check it off the word list

A word-find maze of about two hundred letters is presented with the list of twenty new words. The student visually discriminates among the letters and locates the words by correct letter sequence going across, up, down, or diagonally. The student circles the word and organizes the work by checking off the circled words on the word list. The student is not confused in discrimination and selection of letters because all letters are lowercase.

Exercise 3: Scrambled Eggs

Objectives: • To rearrange twenty sets of letters to make words
  • To write the words in syllables

Twenty sets of letters are presented. By unscrambling the letters and writing them in correct order, the student spells the words correctly. Definitions may be used as aids. After checking the spelling, the student writes the words in syllables and learns how to say the word.

Exercise 4: Pick a Pair

Objective: • To choose the correct definition and write its number in front of the word

Twenty words are listed next to twenty numbered definitions. The student reads the definitions and matches them with the words. The student must visually discriminate among twenty meanings. Since no clues are given, the student must use memory alone.

Exercise 5: Crack the Code

Objectives: • To decode six messages by writing letters under corresponding numbers
  • To create and write a coded message for a partner to decode

Each letter of the alphabet is listed with a corresponding number. Six messages are given in numbered code. The student writes a letter under each number in the messages, using the alphabet-number code. When all the letters in a message are written down, the student determines when one word ends and another begins, to create a meaningful sentence. Then the student writes his or her own sentence and makes it into a coded message. This secret message exercise has the student writing words and creating sentences while having fun.

Exercise 6: Sentence Sense

Objective: • To find and mark one correct sentence in each of the twenty sets of three sentences

Three sentences are given using one of the twenty words. Only one sentence uses the word correctly. The student circles the letter of that sentence. The student considers the meaning of the word in the context of the sentence.

Exercise 7: Pen the Pig

Objective: • To take turns with a partner dictating and spelling words correctly, then connecting dots to form squares

A sheet of about 225 horizontal and vertical dots is given to the student and a partner. Each person has ten words to dictate to the other, taking turns. The words are written on a separate sheet of paper. Each time a person writes a word correctly, he or she draws a line from one dot to another, always hoping to be the last one to complete a square, thus "penning the pig." Each square is initialed by the winner. When students have each written ten words, they switch lists. The game continues until the players have finished switching lists, or until no more dots can be squared. The person with the most squares wins.

The players are writing words. Each is trying to spell correctly to be able to draw a line. This intriguing game motivates each player to spell accurately. When lists are switched, missed words are repeated, promoting longer memory.

Exercise 8: Backward Puzzle

Objectives: • To write a brief definition for each word in the puzzle
• To find and write the hidden sentence that reads from the top down

In this backward puzzle, the student provides the clues. The student must recall the definitions and come up with a few key words for each. To find the hidden sentence, the student separates a string of letters into words, creating a sentence related to the lesson's words.

Exercise 9: Sneaky Snakes

Objective: • To separate run-on letters into twenty words by drawing a line between every word in three timed drills

Three word-snakes are presented on a sheet. The student writes the starting, finishing, and total time it takes to draw slash marks through the snake, slashing after every word. The student tries to decrease his or her time with the second and third word-snakes. The student's eyes must travel rapidly in a left-to-right pattern, stopping after each word. This visual letter sequencing is visual spelling.

Exercise 10: X-ray Vision

Objective: • To write phonetically spelled words correctly and then list them alphabetically

The twenty words are given in phonetic spelling. The student uses visual memory to discover the spelling errors and writes the words correctly on adjoining lines. The student completes the exercise by organizing the words alphabetically on lines that are provided.

Exercise 11: Silly Dilly

Objective: • To write a story using each of the twenty words

A lined sheet with the twenty words listed at the top is presented. Writing a story affords the student an opportunity to use the comprehensive knowledge of these words just gained in an organized and creative way, proving his or her mastery of their spelling and meaning. Satisfactory achievement of this final exercise proves the student has accomplished this lesson's long-term objective.

Word Bankbook

Objectives: • To use the Word Bank Account Bankbook and Word Bank Checks for noting earnings and as proof of earnings
• To act as banker and cancel a check and write the amount earned in the Bankbook
• To note each time the earnings total one thousand dollars, to issue a Preferred Customer Sticker, and to glue it in the Bankbook
• To receive a classroom privilege designated by the teacher for each Preferred Customer Sticker

Each student is given a Word Bankbook showing Word Money earnings. This book gives the student personal pride and shows the student's progress in an appropriate and up-to-date banking-type system. The student and partner have great responsibilities in working the system. This healthy interchange promotes good feelings between peers. The Preferred Customer Sticker is a visible prize. It is handy proof of the number of privileges earned. This type of incentive encourages word study.

Brain Teaser (short-term test)

Objectives: • To write from memory as many words as possible from a lesson unit for a sum of ten Word Money dollars per correct word, and to write the remaining words from dictation for five Word Money dollars per correct word
• To use the Word Banking System to earn Word Money and deposit it in a Word Bank Account
• To write previously missed words to earn Word Money

A sheet is given for a weekly or semimonthly test. The student writes the words from memory to earn ten Word Money dollars for each correctly spelled word. A partner dictates the remaining words, which are worth five dollars per correct word. Missed words are written on the Study Sheets as practice. Then the student can be retested on the missed words to earn more Word Money.

Each time the student's earnings reach one thousand dollars, the banker issues a Preferred Customer Sticker (purchased), which is glued in the Bankbook. This sticker entitles the student to a teacher-designated classroom privilege. The privilege must be worthwhile to motivate the student to increase the earnings.

Monthly Moneymaker (long-term test)

Objective: • To write words from memory and dictation, earning Word Money plus an additional five percent interest on the total earnings as a bonus

This monthly test involves long-term remembering. The five percent bonus motivates the student to practice the words often.

Study Sheets (each student will use several sheets)

Objective: • To write each missed word correctly ten times and then with eyes closed to write it again, mentally "seeing" the word

Study Sheets are given to students as needed to practice words missed on the weekly or monthly tests. After the student writes the words at least ten times each, he or she tries to "see" the word with closed eyes and write it on a line. This technique teaches the student to use visual powers to recall the spelling of a word. The Study Sheets also show the teacher how much the student has practiced.

Word Bank Checks (each student will need several sheets)

Objectives: • To write out checks representing a partner's earnings
  • To read, sign, and deposit a check in a Word Bankbook Account

After taking the Brain Teaser or Monthly Moneymaker tests and figuring how much Word Money has been earned, the banker (partner) writes out a Word Bank Check for the student's total earnings. The student signs the check and gives it to the banker (partner) for deposit in the student's Word Bankbook account. The check system provides for student-partner interchange and responsibility. Besides teaching both people a valuable banking step, it provides a unique method of monitoring learning.

Flash Cards (each student will need five sheets to make twenty cards for a unit)

Objective: • To create a set of flash cards with one vocabulary word on each card, and to say, spell, and define the words in practice sessions

Blank sheets are provided for the student to make his or her own flash cards. The student is involved in creating a personal tool for learning words. The cards may be kept in an envelope at the student's desk for easy access when there are extra minutes to practice.

Classroom Testing Data

This program was tested over a period of nine months with twenty-five students aged twelve to sixteen years. Each student was two or more years below grade level in word knowledge. These students were termed culturally and/or economically deprived. The exercises were completed over 135 minutes weekly per student.

Results indicated seventy to eighty percent accuracy in word meaning and sixty to seventy percent accuracy in spelling.

Vocabulary List

UNIT 1: HOME WORDS

apartment	living room	bathtub	lamp
house	cable	stove	couch
kitchen	video	refrigerator	closet
bedroom	sink	microwave	rug
bathroom	toilet	chair	key

UNIT 2: FOOD WORDS

vegetables	soup	tea	supper
fish	eggs	fruit	cookies
bread	butter	sugar	juice
meat	coffee	breakfast	snack
milk	soda	lunch	cereal

UNIT 3: FAMILY WORDS

mother	children	cousin	husband
father	aunt	grandmother	daughter
sister	uncle	grandfather	son
brother	niece	parents	stepmother
guardian	nephew	wife	stepfather

UNIT 4: TIME WORDS

clock	day	minute	noon
watch	week	second	afternoon
hands	month	A.M.	evening
digital	year	P.M.	night
calendar	hour	morning	date

UNIT 5: FOOD STORE WORDS

supermarket	coupon	aisle	enter
groceries	produce	manager	exit
cart	bakery	clerk	deli
checkout	department	food stamps	receipt
cashier	frozen	brown bag	change

UNIT 6: SCHOOL WORDS

class	fire drill	office	gym
teacher	computer	principal	microchip
period	desk	Internet	board
auditorium	pencil	bell	chalk
cafeteria	paper	software	homework

UNIT 7: HEALTH WORDS

healthy	sore	emergency	nurse
doctor	sprain	vitamin	lab technician
sick	clinic	antiseptic	midwife
ache	hospital	bandage	dentist
hurt	ambulance	appointment	medicine

UNIT 8: COMMUNITY WORDS

factory	synagogue	mall	restaurant
garage	church	mailbox	theater
laundry	police officer	barber	bank
pharmacy	fire station	superintendent	school
sidewalk	post office	plumber	library

UNIT 9: RESTAURANT WORDS

booth	ladies' room	salad	waiter
counter	men's room	sandwich	table
menu	pasta	dessert	espresso
order	reservation	takeout	check
napkin	appetizer	waitress	entrance

UNIT 10: TRAVEL WORDS

bus	subway	conductor	helmet
train	boat	driver	seat belt
cab	bicycle	walk	fare
car	truck	pilot	motorcycle
airplane	ticket	elevator	map

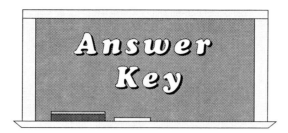

UNIT 1: HOME WORDS

Exercise 1

No answers needed.

Exercise 2

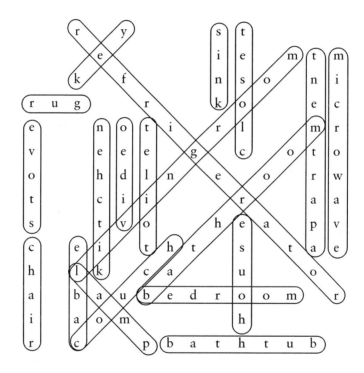

Exercise 3

Syllables

1. apartment	1. a - part - ment
2. house	2. house
3. kitchen	3. kitch - en
4. bedroom	4. bed - room
5. bathroom	5. bath - room
6. living room	6. liv - ing room
7. cable	7. ca - ble
8. video	8. vid - eo
9. sink	9. sink
10. toilet	10. toi - let
11. bathtub	11. bath - tub
12. stove	12. stove
13. refrigerator	13. re - frig - er - a - tor
14. microwave	14. mi - cro - wave
15. chair	15. chair
16. lamp	16. lamp
17. couch	17. couch
18. closet	18. clo - set
19. rug	19. rug
20. key	20. key

Exercise 4

1.	3
2.	7
3.	14
4.	15
5.	10
6.	19
7.	6
8.	20
9.	5
10.	11
11.	4
12.	13
13.	18
14.	1
15.	17
16.	9
17.	16
18.	12
19.	8
20.	2

Exercise 5

We visit in our living room.

The sink is filled with water.

This key will unlock that closet.

The rug on the bedroom floor is blue.

This lamp lights the bathroom.

Our house has many chairs.

Exercise 6

1. c	6. a	11. a	16. b
2. a	7. b	12. c	17. a
3. c	8. c	13. b	18. a
4. a	9. a	14. c	19. b
5. b	10. a	15. a	20. a

Exercise 7

No answers needed.

Exercise 8

1. a bowl with a seat and drain and with a water tank to flush the bowl clean
2. a thick floor mat
3. a seat with a back, for one person
4. a building in which people live
5. a long seat having a back and arms
6. a basin with running water and a drain
7. a room or set of rooms to live in
8. a room where food is cooked

9. an item for cooking and heating food

10. a small room for storing things

11. a tape of a movie, show, or event that is played on a TV set

12. a room in which to take a bath or shower and to use the toilet

13. a large box for keeping food cold

14. a room for general family use

15. an oven that heats and cooks food fast

16. a large tub in which to bathe

17. a TV connection that offers a clear picture and extra programs

18. a room to sleep in

19. an item that gives light

20. a small tool used to lock and unlock

our house is comfortable

Exercises 9 and 10

1. apartment
2. house
3. kitchen
4. bedroom
5. bathroom
6. living rom
7. cable

8. video
9. sink
10. toilet
11. bathtub
12. stove
13. refrigerator
14. microwave

15. chair
16. lamp
17. couch
18. closet
19. rug
20. key

Exercise 10   *Alphabetical Order*

1. apartment
2. bathroom
3. bathtub
4. bedroom
5. cable
6. chair
7. closet

8. couch
9. house
10. key
11. kitchen
12. lamp
13. living room
14. microwave

15. refrigerator
16. rug
17. sink
18. stove
19. toilet
20. video

Exercise 11

No answers needed.

UNIT 2: FOOD WORDS

Exercise 1

No answers needed.

Exercise 2

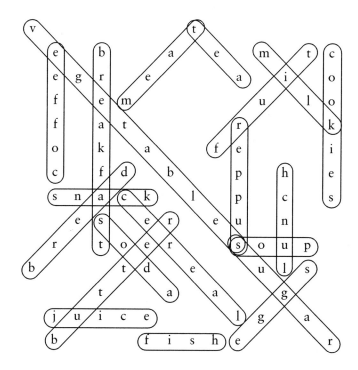

Exercise 3

Syllables

Exercise 4

1. vegetables	1. veg - e -ta - bles	1. 12
2. fish	2. fish	2. 5
3. bread	3. bread	3. 14
4. meat	4. meat	4. 1
5. milk	5. milk	5. 9
6. soup	6. soup	6. 16
7. eggs	7. eggs	7. 17
8. butter	8. but - ter	8. 4
9. coffee	9. cof - fee	9. 18
10. soda	10. so - da	10. 2
11. tea	11. tea	11. 19
12. fruit	12. fruit	12. 7
13. sugar	13. sug - ar	13. 20
14. breakfast	14. break - fast	14. 6
15. lunch	15. lunch	15. 15
16. supper	16. sup - per	16. 10
17. cookies	17. cook - ies	17. 11
18. juice	18. juice	18. 13
19. snack	19. snack	19. 3
20. cereal	20. ce - re - al	20. 8

Exercise 5

These green vegetables are good to eat.

Let's eat supper together.

We had chicken, fruit, and milk for lunch.

Breakfast can be juice, cereal, and milk.

Please put butter on your bread.

We had three cookies for a snack.

Exercise 6

1. c	6. a	11. b	16. a
2. c	7. c	12. a	17. c
3. c	8. c	13. b	18. b
4. a	9. a	14. b	19. a
5. b	10. b	15. b	20. b

Exercise 7

No answers needed.

Exercise 8

1. the first meal of the day
2. a food made of grain
3. hard-shelled food produced by chickens
4. the liquid of fruit and other foods
5. a solid food made by churning milk or cream
6. plants that can be eaten
7. a drink made by pouring boiling water over dried leaves
8. a dark brown drink made from the beans of a particular tree
9. the last meal of the day
10. animal tissue used for food
11. part of a plant that has seeds and can be eaten
12. a white material taken from cane or beet and used to sweeten food
13. small flat cakes
14. a liquid food with meat, fish, or vegetables as a base
15. a sweet drink made of soda water and flavoring
16. a white liquid often used to feed babies
17. a baked food made mainly of flour
18. a small amount of food eaten between meals
19. the second or noon meal of the day
20. the flesh of an underwater animal used for food

be sure to eat good meals

Exercises 9 and 10

1. vegetables
2. fish
3. bread
4. meat
5. milk
6. soup
7. eggs
8. butter
9. coffee
10. soda
11. tea
12. fruit
13. sugar
14. breakfast
15. lunch
16. supper
17. cookies
18. juice
19. snack
20. cereal

Exercise 10   Alphabetical Order

1. bread
2. breakfast
3. butter
4. cereal
5. coffee
6. cookies
7. eggs

8. fish
9. fruit
10. juice
11. lunch
12. meat
13. milk
14. snack

15. soda
16. soup
17. sugar
18. supper
19. tea
20. vegetables

Exercise 11

No answers needed.

UNIT 3: FAMILY WORDS

Exercise 1

No answers needed.

Exercise 2

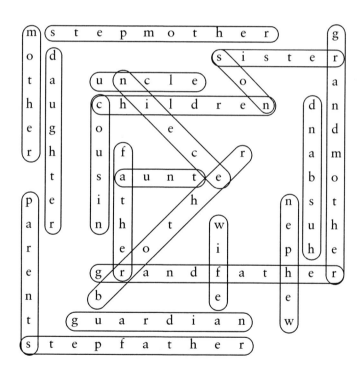

Exercise 3

Syllables

1. mother	1. moth - er
2. father	2. fa - ther
3. sister	3. sis - ter
4. brother	4. broth - er
5. guardian	5. guard - ian
6. children	6. chil - dren
7. aunt	7. aunt
8. uncle	8. un - cle
9. niece	9. niece
10. nephew	10. neph - ew
11. cousin	11. cou - sin
12. grandmother	12. grand - moth - er
13. grandfather	13. grand - fath - er
14. parents	14. par - ents
15. wife	15. wife
16. husband	16. hus - band
17. daughter	17. daugh - ter
18. son	18. son
19. stepmother	19. step - moth - er
20. stepfather	20. step - fath - er

Exercise 4

1. 14	11. 15
2. 12	12. 16
3. 9	13. 13
4. 10	14. 20
5. 2	15. 11
6. 8	16. 19
7. 4	17. 18
8. 3	18. 6
9. 7	19. 17
10. 1	20. 5

Exercise 5

My father is a smart man.

Those children are playing ball.

My parents take care of me.

Your sister knows my brother.

Their daughter is a tall girl.

My aunt and uncle live with us.

Exercise 6

1. a	6. b	11. a	16. b
2. b	7. a	12. b	17. c
3. a	8. a	13. a	18. b
4. c	9. a	14. c	19. a
5. b	10. b	15. c	20. a

Exercise 7

No answers needed.

Exercise 8

1. a woman who has borne a child
2. a person's female child
3. the brother of your father or mother
4. a man or boy related to you by having the same parents
5. the father of your father or mother
6. the sister of your father or mother
7. a woman married to your father after the death or divorce of your mother
8. the daughter of your sister or brother

9. sons and daughters in a family
10. a person appointed to take care of another
11. a person's male child
12. the mother of your father or mother
13. the son or daughter of your uncle or aunt
14. a woman to whom a man is married
15. a man married to your mother after the death or divorce of your father
16. a male parent
17. a father and mother
18. the son of your sister or brother
19. a man to whom a woman is married
20. a woman or girl related to you by having the same parents

each family is different

Exercises 9 and 10

1. mother	8. uncle	15. wife
2. father	9. niece	16. husband
3. sister	10. nephew	17. daughter
4. brother	11. cousin	18. son
5. guardian	12. grandmother	19. stepmother
6. children	13. grandfather	20. stepfather
7. aunt	14. parents	

Exercise 10   Alphabetical Order

1. aunt	8. grandmother	15. sister
2. brother	9. guardian	16. son
3. children	10. husband	17. stepfather
4. cousin	11. mother	18. stepmother
5. daughter	12. nephew	19. uncle
6. father	13. niece	20. wife
7. grandfather	14. parents	

Exercise 11

No answers needed.

UNIT 4: TIME WORDS

Exercise 1

No answers needed.

Exercise 2

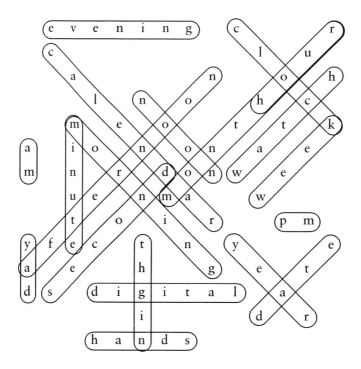

Exercise 3

Syllables

1. clock	1. clock
2. watch	2. watch
3. hands	3. hands
4. digital	4. dig - i - tal
5. calendar	5. cal - en - dar
6. day	6. day
7. week	7. week
8. month	8. month
9. year	9. year
10. hour	10. hour
11. minute	11. min - ute
12. second	12. sec - ond
13. A.M.	13. A.M.
14. P.M.	14. P.M.
15. morning	15. morn - ing
16. noon	16. noon
17. afternoon	17. af - ter - noon
18. evening	18. eve - ning
19. night	19. night
20. date	20. date

Exercise 4

1. 6
2. 9
3. 2
4. 12
5. 16
6. 18
7. 5
8. 1
9. 14
10. 15
11. 8
12. 20
13. 4
14. 10
15. 19
16. 17
17. 11
18. 13
19. 7
20. 3

Exercise 5

I wear my watch on my wrist.

Look at the clock to see the time.

We have breakfast in the morning.

Our company came to supper.

The calendar hangs on the wall.

We watch TV in the evening.

Exercise 6

1. b	6. a	11. a	16. b
2. a	7. b	12. b	17. a
3. b	8. b	13. a	18. b
4. a	9. b	14. c	19. b
5. c	10. a	15. b	20. a

Exercise 7

No answers needed.

Exercise 8

1. time shown in numbers
2. the period of time from sunset to sunrise
3. before noon
4. seven days
5. a period of four weeks or about thirty days
6. the last part of the day and the early part of the night
7. an item for measuring time by means of pointers moving over a dial or by progressing numbers, usually not worn or carried by the user
8. after noon
9. pointers on a clock
10. one time unit—twenty-four of these units make one day
11. one time unit—sixty of these units make one minute
12. a chart showing the days, weeks, and months of a year
13. an item for measuring time, which is worn or carried by the user
14. the first part of the day from dawn to noon
15. the middle of the day at twelve o'clock
16. one time unit—sixty of these units make one hour
17. the time from noon to evening
18. a period of twenty-four hours, or the period of light between sunrise and sunset
19. the time at which a thing happens
20. twelve months

time helps us plan our day

Exercises 9 and 10

1. clock	8. month	15. morning
2. watch	9. year	16. noon
3. hands	10. hour	17. afternoon
4. digital	11. minute	18. evening
5. calendar	12. second	19. night
6. day	13. A.M.	20. date
7. week	14. P.M.	

Exercise 10   Alphabetical Order

1. afternoon
2. A.M.
3. calendar
4. clock
5. date
6. day
7. digital
8. evening
9. hands
10. hour
11. minute
12. month
13. morning
14. night
15. noon
16. P.M.
17. second
18. watch
19. week
20. year

Exercise 11

No answers needed.

UNIT 5: FOOD STORE WORDS

Exercise 1

No answers needed.

Exercise 2

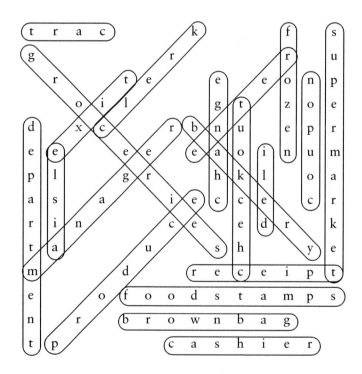

Exercise 3

Syllables

1.	supermarket	1. su - per - mar - ket
2.	groceries	2. gro - cer - ies
3.	cart	3. cart
4.	checkout	4. check - out
5.	cashier	5. cash - ier
6.	coupon	6. cou - pon
7.	produce	7. pro - duce
8.	bakery	8. bak - er - y
9.	department	9. de - part - ment
10.	frozen	10. fro - zen
11.	aisle	11. aisle
12.	manager	12. man - ag - er
13.	clerk	13. clerk
14.	food stamps	14. food stamps
15.	brown bag	15. brown bag
16.	enter	16. en - ter
17.	exit	17. ex - it
18.	deli	18. del - i
19.	receipt	19. re - ceipt
20.	change	20. change

Exercise 4

1. 8
2. 10
3. 15
4. 1
5. 18
6. 16
7. 6
8. 19
9. 3
10. 11
11. 4
12. 2
13. 20
14. 9
15. 17
16. 5
17. 13
18. 14
19. 7
20. 12

Exercise 5

Let's shop for groceries.

The cashier will take our money.

Put the frozen food down.

The bakery is on this aisle.

We need a brown bag for the produce.

He bought meat at the deli.

Exercise 6

1. a	6. b	11. c	16. c
2. c	7. b	12. a	17. c
3. a	8. a	13. a	18. b
4. b	9. a	14. b	19. a
5. a	10. b	15. a	20. c

Exercise 7

No answers needed.

xxiv   Survival Vocabulary

Exercise 8

1. a paper holder in which to put groceries and other items
2. to go in or come in
3. a person who sells in a store
4. a way out
5. a place where bread and pastries are sold
6. a large store selling food and other goods
7. a walkway between rows of stacked items
8. a person in charge of money
9. a ticket used to get money off the price of an item
10. crops grown by a farmer
11. a section of a store
12. a slip of paper marked with the amount paid
13. money owed to a buyer who pays more than is due
14. a person in charge
15. a counter where groceries are paid for
16. a container used to carry groceries
17. as cold and as hard as ice
18. food and household items
19. paper issued to people for use as cash to buy food
20. a place where prepared and cooked foods are sold

we like shopping for food

Exercises 9 and 10

1. supermarket
2. groceries
3. cart
4. checkout
5. cashier
6. coupon
7. produce
8. bakery
9. department
10. frozen
11. aisle
12. manager
13. clerk
14. food stamps
15. brown bag
16. enter
17. exit
18. deli
19. receipt
20. change

Exercise 10   Alphabetical Order

1. aisle
2. bakery
3. brown bag
4. cart
5. cashier
6. change
7. checkout
8. clerk
9. coupon
10. deli
11. department
12. enter
13. exit
14. food stamps
15. frozen
16. groceries
17. manager
18. produce
19. receipt
20. supermarket

Exercise 11

No answers needed.

UNIT 6: SCHOOL WORDS

Exercise 1

No answers needed.

Exercise 2

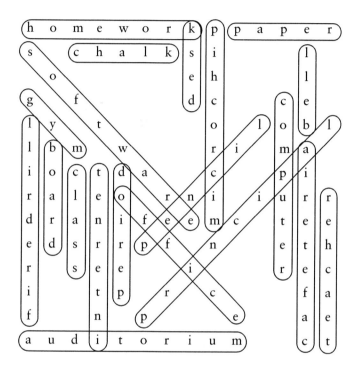

Exercise 3

Syllables

1. class	1. class
2. teacher	2. teach - er
3. period	3. pe - ri - od
4. auditorium	4. au - di - to - ri - um
5. cafeteria	5. caf - e - te - ri - a
6. fire drill	6. fire drill
7. computer	7. com - put - er
8. desk	8. desk
9. pencil	9. pen - cil
10. paper	10. pa - per
11. office	11. of - fice
12. principal	12. prin - ci- pal
13. Internet	13. In - ter - net
14. bell	14. bell
15. software	15. soft - ware
16. gym	16. gym
17. microchip	17. mi - cro - chip
18. board	18. board
19. chalk	19. chalk
20. homework	20. home - work

Exercise 4

1. 3	11. 1
2. 9	12. 13
3. 7	13. 12
4. 14	14. 18
5. 20	15. 16
6. 10	16. 8
7. 2	17. 15
8. 17	18. 11
9. 5	19. 4
10. 19	20. 6

Exercise 5

The class will line up when the fire drill begins.

Put the paper and pencil on the desk.

The teacher writes on the board with chalk.

The auditorium is next to the gym.

We eat in the cafeteria.

The principal and the nurse are in the office.

Exercise 6

1. b	6. b	11. c	16. a
2. a	7. a	12. c	17. c
3. b	8. a	13. a	18. b
4. c	9. b	14. b	19. c
5. c	10. a	15. c	20. a

Exercise 7

No answers needed.

Exercise 8

1. a large room for games and exercise; also, physical education class
2. a place where most of the paperwork is done for a school or a business
3. a machine that processes and stores information
4. a pointed tool to write with
5. practice leaving the building in case of fire
6. a person who gives instruction or shows how to do something
7. a huge computer network where information can be found and shared
8. the head person in a school

9. a flat, dark surface for writing on with chalk

10. something that makes a ringing sound

11. schoolwork done at home

12. the program or instructions that tell a computer what to do

13. a thin sheet used for writing or printing

14. a large dining area where people buy food at a counter and carry it to a table to eat

15. a piece of furniture with a flat top on which to write

16. a tiny square of thin material used in electronic equipment

17. soft, white limestone used to write with

18. a portion of time; also, a dot at the end of a sentence

19. a large room where groups of people can meet

20. a group of students taught together

you learn a lot at school

Exercises 9 and 10

1. class
2. teacher
3. period
4. auditorium
5. cafeteria
6. fire drill
7. computer

8. desk
9. pencil
10. paper
11. office
12. principal
13. Internet
14. bell

15. software
16. gym
17. microchip
18. board
19. chalk
20. homework

Exercise 10   Alphabetical Order

1. auditorium
2. bell
3. board
4. cafeteria
5. chalk
6. class
7. computer

8. desk
9. fire drill
10. gym
11. homework
12. Internet
13. microchip
14. office

15. paper
16. pencil
17. period
18. principal
19. software
20. teacher

Exercise 11

No answers needed.

UNIT 7: HEALTH WORDS

Exercise 1

No answers needed.

Exercise 2

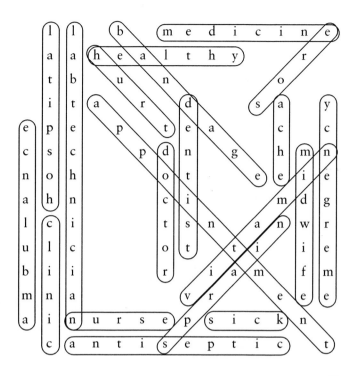

Exercise 3   Exercise 4

Syllables

1. healthy	1. health - y	1. 9
2. doctor	2. doc - tor	2. 2
3. sick	3. sick	3. 8
4. ache	4. ache	4. 12
5. hurt	5. hurt	5. 1
6. sore	6. sore	6. 6
7. sprain	7. sprain	7. 10
8. clinic	8. clin - ic	8. 17
9. hospital	9. hos - pi - tal	9. 4
10. ambulance	10. am - bu - lance	10. 11
11. emergency	11. e - mer - gen - cy	11. 16
12. vitamin	12. vi - ta - min	12. 18
13. antiseptic	13. an - ti- sep - tic	13. 15
14. bandage	14. band - age	14. 5
15. appointment	15. ap - point - ment	15. 19
16. nurse	16. nurse	16. 14
17. lab technician	17. lab tech - ni - cian	17. 20
18. midwife	18. mid - wife	18. 7
19. dentist	19. den - tist	19. 13
20. medicine	20. med - i - cine	20. 3

Exercise 5

Eat good food to be healthy.

Sick people see a doctor for help.

Cover a cut with a bandage.

Take the medicine as the dentist said.

Make the appointment for two o'clock.

Go the the clinic if your throat is still sore.

Exercise 6

1. a	6. a	11. a	16. c
2. b	7. c	12. a	17. b
3. a	8. a	13. b	18. c
4. c	9. b	14. b	19. a
5. a	10. a	15. a	20. b

Exercise 7

No answers needed.

Exercise 8

1. something that kills germs
2. a place where sick people are cared for and may stay overnight
3. a person trained to treat people who are sick or hurt
4. having some illness or disease
5. to have pain
6. a person who takes care of the sick
7. a van for bringing sick or injured people to the hospital
8. being well; a good condition of the body
9. a doctor whose work is caring for teeth
10. a person who tests blood and other samples
11. painful
12. a substance needed for normal body growth and health
13. something serious that happens suddenly and calls for fast action
14. an injury caused by sudden twisting
15. a person who helps women give birth
16. something to help improve or cure an illness or disease
17. a cover for a cut or other injury
18. a place where sick people are treated and released
19. an arrangement to be somewhere at a certain time
20. a dull pain that lasts for a while

pick health over wealth

Exercises 9 and 10

1. healthy
2. doctor
3. sick
4. ache
5. hurt
6. sore
7. sprain
8. clinic
9. hospital
10. ambulance
11. emergency
12. vitamin
13. antiseptic
14. bandage
15. appointment
16. nurse
17. lab technician
18. midwife
19. dentist
20. medicine

Exercise 10   Alphabetical Order

1. ache
2. ambulance
3. antiseptic
4. appointment
5. bandage
6. clinic
7. dentist
8. doctor
9. emergency
10. healthy
11. hospital
12. hurt
13. lab technician
14. medicine
15. midwife
16. nurse
17. sick
18. sore
19. sprain
20. vitamin

Exercise 11

No answers needed.

UNIT 8: COMMUNITY WORDS

Exercise 1

No answers needed.

Exercise 2

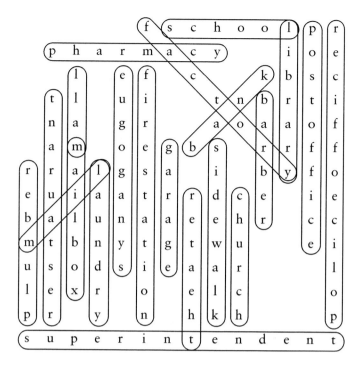

Exercise 3

Syllables

1. factory	1. fac - to - ry	
2. garage	2. ga - rage	
3. laundry	3. laun - dry	
4. pharmacy	4. phar - ma - cy	
5. sidewalk	5. side - walk	
6. synagogue	6. syn - a - gogue	
7. church	7. church	
8. police officer	8. po - lice of - fi - cer	
9. fire station	9. fire sta - tion	
10. post office	10. post of - fice	
11. mall	11. mall	
12. mailbox	12. mail - box	
13. barber	13. bar - ber	
14. superintendent	14. su - per - in - tend - ent	
15. plumber	15. plumb - er	
16. restaurant	16. res - tau - rant	
17. theater	17. the - a - ter	
18. bank	18. bank	
19. school	19. school	
20. library	20. li - brar - y	

Exercise 4

1. 7
2. 14
3. 15
4. 4
5. 1
6. 16
7. 8
8. 11
9. 17
10. 2
11. 10
12. 20
13. 19
14. 9
15. 3
16. 18
17. 6
18. 13
19. 12
20. 5

Exercise 5

We take our sheets to that laundry.

That theater is showing a funny film.

Our library has so many books.

That police officer stopped the fight.

There is a large garage next to the factory.

We ride a bus to get to school.

Exercise 6

1. b	6. c	11. c	16. a
2. a	7. a	12. c	17. a
3. c	8. b	13. a	18. b
4. c	9. c	14. c	19. c
5. a	10. a	15. b	20. a

Exercise 7

No answers needed.

Exercise 8

1. a building where cars are parked or repaired
2. a person who cuts other people's hair
3. a building for people and equipment that put out fires
4. a place where movies are shown
5. a place for teaching and learning
6. a place for saving, borrowing, or exchanging money
7. a place where clothes and linens are washed
8. a person who keeps order
9. a place at the side of a street where people can walk
10. a place to buy and eat a meal
11. a building where Christians worship
12. a place where things are made
13. a building where Jews worship
14. a large building containing a variety of shops
15. a store where medicine is sold
16. a person who installs and repairs pipes
17. a person who oversees something or is in charge of an apartment building
18. a box from which mail is collected or to which mail is delivered
19. a place where mail is handled and postage stamps are sold
20. a place where many books are kept

get to know the community

Exercises 9 and 10

1. factory
2. garage
3. laundry
4. pharmacy
5. sidewalk
6. synagogue
7. church
8. police officer
9. fire station
10. post office
11. mall
12. mailbox
13. barber
14. superintendent
15. plumber
16. restaurant
17. theater
18. bank
19. school
20. library

Exercise 10   *Alphabetical Order*

1. bank
2. barber
3. church
4. factory
5. fire station
6. garage
7. laundry
8. library
9. mailbox
10. mall
11. pharmacy
12. plumber
13. police officer
14. post office
15. restaurant
16. school
17. sidewalk
18. superintendent
19. synagogue
20. theater

Exercise 11

No answers needed.

UNIT 9: RESTAURANT WORDS

Exercise 1

No answers needed.

Exercise 2

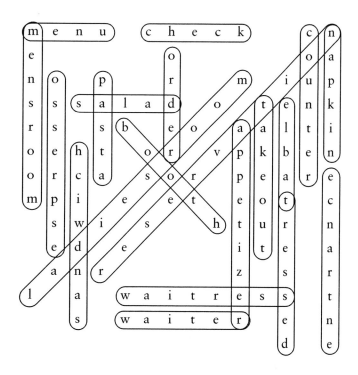

Exercise 3

Syllables

1. booth	1. booth
2. counter	2. count - er
3. menu	3. men - u
4. order	4. or - der
5. napkin	5. nap - kin
6. ladies' room	6. la - dies' room
7. men's room	7. men's room
8. pasta	8. pas - ta
9. reservation	9. res - er - va - tion
10. appetizer	10. ap - pe - tiz - er
11. salad	11. sal - ad
12. sandwich	12. sand - wich
13. dessert	13. des - sert
14. takeout	14. take - out
15. waitress	15. wait - ress
16. waiter	16. wait - er
17. table	17. ta - ble
18. espresso	18. es - pres - so
19. check	19. check
20. entrance	20. en - trance

Exercise 4

1. 5
2. 18
3. 6
4. 17
5. 20
6. 16
7. 12
8. 3
9. 19
10. 14
11. 9
12. 8
13. 1
14. 10
15. 15
16. 11
17. 13
18. 4
19. 7
20. 2

Exercise 5

I made a reservation.

That booth is empty.

The waitress has our order.

I love dessert.

Is our check ready yet?

The table is near the entrance.

Exercise 6

1. b	6. a	11. c	16. a
2. a	7. a	12. a	17. b
3. c	8. a	13. a	18. c
4. a	9. a	14. a	19. c
5. b	10. a	15. c	20. b

Exercise 7

No answers needed.

Exercise 8

1. food eaten before a meal to increase the desire for more food
2. a folded cloth or paper used at meals for protecting clothing and for wiping lips or fingers
3. a partly enclosed space with a table and seats for several people
4. food removed from a restaurant and eaten somewhere else
5. a long table
6. a man who serves food
7. a piece of furniture having a flat top on legs

8. a list of food served in a restaurant

9. a serving of food asked for in a restaurant

10. a place through which a person goes in or comes in

11. an arrangement to have a table ready for a person

12. a bathroom for men and boys

13. a bathroom for women and girls

14. slices of bread with a filling between them

15. a dish of cooked macaroni, spaghetti, or such

16. a dish of raw vegetables

17. coffee brewed by forcing steam through dark roasted beans

18. a woman who serves food

19. a written statement of the amount owed in a restaurant

20. food eaten at the end of a meal

eat out and try new tastes

Exercises 9 and 10

1. booth
2. counter
3. menu
4. order
5. napkin
6. ladies' room
7. men's room
8. pasta
9. reservation
10. appetizer
11. salad
12. sandwich
13. dessert
14. takeout
15. waitress
16. waiter
17. table
18. espresso
19. check
20. entrance

Exercise 10   Alphabetical Order

1. appetizer
2. booth
3. check
4. counter
5. dessert
6. entrance
7. espresso
8. ladies' room
9. men's room
10. menu
11. napkin
12. order
13. pasta
14. reservation
15. salad
16. sandwich
17. table
18. takeout
19. waiter
20. waitress

Exercise 11

No answers needed.

UNIT 10: TRAVEL WORDS

Exercise 1

No answers needed.

Exercise 2

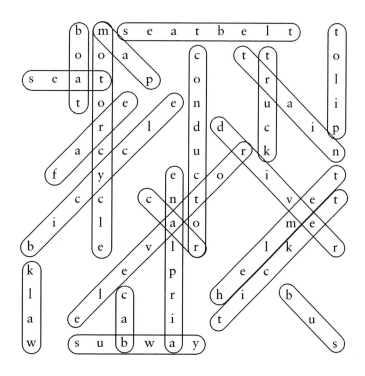

Exercise 3

Syllables

1. bus
2. train
3. cab
4. car
5. airplane
6. subway
7. boat
8. bicycle
9. truck
10. ticket
11. conductor
12. driver
13. walk
14. pilot
15. elevator
16. helmet
17. seat belt
18. fare
19. motorcycle
20. map

1. bus
2. train
3. cab
4. car
5. air - plane
6. sub - way
7. boat
8. bi - cy - cle
9. truck
10. tick - et
11. con - duc - tor
12. driv - er
13. walk
14. pi - lot
15. el - e - va - tor
16. hel - met
17. seat belt
18. fare
19. mo - tor - cy - cle
20. map

Exercise 4

1. 12
2. 7
3. 14
4. 15
5. 16
6. 1
7. 19
8. 20
9. 3
10. 6
11. 18
12. 2
13. 13
14. 9
15. 17
16. 11
17. 4
18. 5
19. 10
20. 8

Exercise 5

The conductor waved to us from the train.

That motorcycle belongs to me.

I paid my fare to ride on the bus.

That airplane carries many people.

I ride on the subway every day of the week.

The elevator will take us up.

Exercise 6

1. a	6. a	11. c	16. a
2. c	7. b	12. a	17. b
3. b	8. a	13. b	18. a
4. a	9. a	14. b	19. b
5. b	10. a	15. a	20. a

Exercise 7

No answers needed.

Exercise 8

1. to move along on foot
2. a watercraft moved by oars, sails, or engine
3. a person who flies an airplane or steers a boat
4. a small printed card that gives a person a specific right
5. the amount of money paid for a ride
6. a two-wheeled vehicle moved by an engine, larger and heavier than a bicycle
7. a four-wheeled motor vehicle driven on streets
8. a machine with wings that flies in the air
9. a protective covering for the head
10. a chart that shows roads, cities, and other surface features
11. a car for public use with a driver who is paid
12. a small cage-like room that moves people from floor to floor in tall buildings
13. an underground electric railway
14. a vehicle for hauling loads along the streets
15. a person in charge of passengers who collects fares
16. a person who makes a vehicle move
17. a line of connected railroad cars on a track, pulled or pushed by a locomotive
18. a large motor vehicle that can carry many people and usually follows a regular route
19. a vehicle to ride on with two wheels, handlebars, a seat, and foot pedals to move it
20. a strap that holds a person in a seat

look for places to visit

Exercises 9 and 10

1. bus
2. train
3. cab
4. car
5. airplane
6. subway
7. boat
8. bicycle
9. truck
10. ticket
11. conductor
12. driver
13. walk
14. pilot
15. elevator
16. helmet
17. seat belt
18. fare
19. motorcycle
20. map

Exercise 10   Alphabetical Order

1. airplane
2. bicycle
3. boat
4. bus
5. cab
6. car
7. conductor
8. driver
9. elevator
10. fare
11. helmet
12. map
13. motorcycle
14. pilot
15. seat belt
16. subway
17. ticket
18. train
19. truck
20. walk

Exercise 11

No answers needed.

Unit 1
Home Words

apartment

house

bathtub

kitchen

bedroom

chair

lamp

living room

key

sink

cable

closet

stove

refrigerator

microwave

bathroom

couch

rug

video

toilet

Survival Vocabulary

New Words and Lost Letters

Read each word and its definition. In the Lost Letters column, write each word by filling in the missing letters.

LOST LETTERS

1.	apartment	a room or set of rooms to live in	_ p _ _ tm _ _ t
2.	house	a building in which people live	h _ _ se
3.	kitchen	a room where food is cooked	_ i _ _ _ en
4.	bedroom	a room to sleep in	b _ dr _ _ m
5.	bathroom	a room in which to take a bath or shower and to use the toilet	b _ _ _ ro _ _
6.	living room	a room for general family use	_ _ v _ _ g r _ _ m
7.	cable	a TV connection that offers a clear picture and extra programs	c _ b _ e
8.	video	a tape of a movie, show, or event that is played on a TV set	_ _ d e _
9.	sink	a basin with running water and a drain	s _ _ k
10.	toilet	a bowl with a seat and drain and with a water tank to flush the bowl clean	to _ _ _ t
11.	bathtub	a large tub in which to bathe	b _ th _ _ _
12.	stove	an item for cooking and heating food	s _ _ _ _
13.	refrigerator	a large box for keeping food cold	r _ f _ i _ e _ a _ _ _
14.	microwave	an oven that heats and cooks food fast	mi _ r _ w _ ve
15.	chair	a seat with a back, for one person	c _ _ i _
16.	lamp	an item that gives light	l _ _ _
17.	couch	a long seat having a back and arms	co _ _ h
18.	closet	a small room for storing things	cl _ _ _ _
19.	rug	a thick floor mat	r _ _
20.	key	a small tool used to lock and unlock	k _ y

Survival Vocabulary

Name _____

Date _____

Snoop and Solve

Find the words in the maze and circle them. The words may go across, up, down, or diagonally. Check them off in the list at the top as you find them.

___ 1. apartment	___ 8. video	___ 15. chair
___ 2. house	___ 9. sink	___ 16. lamp
___ 3. kitchen	___ 10. toilet	___ 17. couch
___ 4. bedroom	___ 11. bathtub	___ 18. closet
___ 5. bathroom	___ 12. stove	___ 19. rug
___ 6. living room	___ 13. refrigerator	___ 20. key
___ 7. cable	___ 14. microwave	

k	l	r	u	y	n	o	r	s	t	a	i	r	s
e	m	c	e	f	a	p	u	i	e	a	m	t	m
e	v	k	k	f	m	r	j	n	s	o	b	n	i
r	u	g	a	r	r	s	g	k	o	r	d	e	c
e	o	f	n	o	t	i	b	r	l	h	u	m	r
v	o	g	e	e	e	n	g	a	c	h	o	t	o
o	r	y	h	d	l	n	t	e	t	o	b	r	w
t	e	a	c	i	i	g	e	a	r	t	o	a	a
s	f	w	t	v	o	c	m	h	e	a	t	p	v
c	g	e	i	o	t	h	t	o	s	h	t	a	e
h	e	l	k	m	c	a	s	e	u	i	t	o	e
a	r	b	a	u	b	e	d	r	o	o	m	r	r
i	a	a	o	m	l	e	t	c	h	l	b	n	a
r	t	c	o	u	p	b	a	t	h	t	u	b	c

Survival Vocabulary

Scrambled Eggs

Write the words correctly.	Divide the words into syllables.

1. parmenatt _____ _____

2. huose _____ _____

3. kichtne _____ _____

4. bdermoo _____ _____

5. rmoothba _____ _____

6. vilgin romo _____ _____

7. bleac _____ _____

8. doive _____ _____

9. nisk _____ _____

10. ittleo _____ _____

11. thtbaub _____ _____

12. evost _____ _____

13. frreigertaor _____ _____

14. revimowac _____ _____

15. airhc _____ _____

16. pmla _____ _____

17. hocuc _____ _____

18. setocl _____ _____

19. gru _____ _____

20. yke _____ _____

Name _____

Date _____

Pick a Pair

Write the number of each definition in front of the word it goes with.

____ apartment	1. an oven that heats and cooks food fast
____ house	2. a small tool used to lock and unlock
____ kitchen	3. a room or set of rooms to live in
____ bedroom	4. a large tub in which to bathe
____ bathroom	5. a basin with running water and a drain
____ living room	6. a TV connection that offers a clear picture and extra programs
____ cable	7. a building in which people live
____ video	8. a thick floor mat
____ sink	9. an item that gives light
____ toilet	10. a room in which to take a bath or shower and to use the toilet
____ bathtub	11. a bowl with a seat and drain and with a water tank to flush the bowl clean
____ stove	12. a small room for storing things
____ refrigerator	13. an item for cooking and heating food
____ microwave	14. a room where food is cooked
____ chair	15. a room to sleep in
____ lamp	16. a long seat having a back and arms
____ couch	17. a seat with a back, for one person
____ closet	18. a large box for keeping food cold
____ rug	19. a room for general family use
____ key	20. a tape of a movie, show, or event that is played on a TV set

Survival Vocabulary

Name _____

Date _____

Crack the Code

1 - a	6 - f	11 - k	16 - p	21 - u	24 - x
2 - b	7 - g	12 - l	17 - q	22 - v	25 - y
3 - c	8 - h	13 - m	18 - r	23 - w	26 - z
4 - d	9 - i	14 - n	19 - s		
5 - e	10 - j	15 - o	20 - t		

Write the letters under the numbers below to crack the code.

23 - 5 - 22 - 9 - 19 - 9 - 20 - 9 - 14 - 15 - 21 - 18 - 12 - 9 - 22 - 9 - 14 - 7 - 18 - 15- 15 - 13.

20 - 8 - 5 - 19 - 9 - 14 - 11 - 9 - 19 - 6 - 9 - 12 - 12 - 5 - 4 - 23 - 9 - 20 - 8 - 23 - 1 - 20 - 5 - 18

20 - 8 - 9 - 19 - 11 - 5 - 25 - 23 - 9 - 12 - 12 - 21 - 14 - 12 - 15 - 3 - 11 - 20 - 8 - 1 - 20 - 3- 12 -

15 - 19 - 5 - 20.

20 - 8 - 5 - 18 - 21 - 7 - 15 - 14 - 20 - 8 - 5 - 2 - 5 - 4 - 18 - 15 - 15 - 13 - 6 - 12 - 15 - 15 - 18 -

9 - 19 - 2 - 12 - 21 - 5.

20 - 8 - 9 - 19 - 12 - 1 - 13 - 16 - 12 - 9 - 7 - 8 - 20 - 19 - 20 - 8 - 5 - 2 - 1 - 20 - 8 - 18 - 15 -

15 - 13.

15 - 21 - 18 - 8 - 15 - 21 - 19 - 5 - 8 - 1 - 19 - 13 - 1 - 14 - 25 - 3 - 8 - 1 - 9 - 18 - 19.

On the back of this page, write your own coded message. Ask your partner to
crack it.

Survival Vocabulary

Sentence Sense

Read each sentence. One of the three sentences sounds correct. Circle the letter in front of the correct sentence.

1. (a) I climb up the apartment to get to our front door.
   (b) My father puts our apartment in the washer to clean it.
   (c) Our apartment is on the third floor.

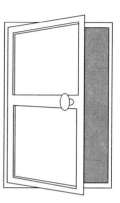

2. (a) Our family lives in a large brown house.
   (b) The house that covers the floor is nice and soft.
   (c) Please put some house in the tub to wash clothes.

3. (a) He put the kitchen in the door lock to open it.
   (b) Now we can kitchen the food for supper.
   (c) Our family eats breakfast at the table in the kitchen.

4. (a) His brother sleeps in the same bedroom that he does.
   (b) The bedroom in the bathroom is for taking a bath.
   (c) Please bedroom all of your clothes before going to school.

5. (a) Please help me move the lamp and couch into the bathroom.
   (b) The sink and toilet are in the bathroom.
   (c) Our family eats dinner in the bathroom every evening.

6. (a) Our family visits with company in our living room.
   (b) The water I poured in the living room is to wash clothes.
   (c) Let's spread the living room on the floor to cover it.

7. (a) Please wait at the top of the key for my cable.
   (b) Check to see if the program is on cable.
   (c) I will cook all of the cable for our supper.

8. (a) Many people are walking down this long video in school.
   (b) Try to fit the door in the video so we can open it.
   (c) Please sit down and I will turn on the video.

9. (a) The sink is a good place to wash all those dishes.
   (b) He wants to sink the stove so it will get warm.
   (c) Our family lives in that big sink on the corner.

(continued)

Survival Vocabulary

Sentence Sense (continued)

10. (a) Ask her little sister if she would like to use the toilet.
    (b) Try to put the toilet in his refrigerator.
    (c) She fit all of her clothes in the large toilet in her bedroom.

11. (a) I love to bathe in the bathtub before I go to bed.
    (b) Don't bathtub that chair next to the stove.
    (c) Our stove is in the bathtub so we may cook on it.

12. (a) Be careful when you go up and down the stove.
    (b) We visit with our company in the stove where we have room.
    (c) My mother has a nice new stove to use to cook our meals.

13. (a) We use our refrigerator to wash all of our clothes.
    (b) Milk and other food must be kept cold in the refrigerator.
    (c) This blue refrigerator looks nice on my sister's bed.

14. (a) Many of my friends can sit on the microwave in our living room.
    (b) He couldn't fit the microwave in the lock of the door.
    (c) Please help me reheat the food in the microwave.

15. (a) Please get a chair for my father to sit on.
    (b) Our food stays cold in that chair.
    (c) Please turn on the chair so I can make some tea.

16. (a) The lamp on this ring is to open that door.
    (b) He turned on the lamp when it got dark in the room.
    (c) We use a big lamp to cook our food on.

17. (a) Lots of people can sit on the couch in our living room.
    (b) Please help me move the couch into the washer.
    (c) Our family lives in the brown couch on the next street.

18. (a) He can hang all of his clothes in this big closet.
    (b) Please closet all the vegetables before you cook them.
    (c) Our company can visit in the closet while they are here.

19. (a) She tried to fit the rug into the lock to open the door.
    (b) Please help me spread this big rug on the bedroom floor.
    (c) He wants you to turn on the rug because it's dark now.

20. (a) I can fit this little key in my pocket.
    (b) His father wants us to key the meat for supper.
    (c) Let's key the clothes and hang them out to dry.

Pen the Pig

1. Divide the list of words in Exercise 1 into two lists of ten words each.
2. Choose a partner. Give your partner one of the lists of ten words. You keep the other list.
3. Say one of the words on your list. Your partner writes it down on a sheet of paper.
4. You check your partner's spelling.
5. If the word is spelled correctly, your partner may touch his or her pencil to a dot and draw one straight line across or down to another dot.
6. If the word is not spelled correctly, your partner may not draw a line.
7. Now your partner says one of the words on his or her list to you. You write it down.
8. Your partner checks the spelling.
9. If the word is spelled correctly, you may draw one line between two dots, going across or down.
10. If the word is not spelled correctly, you may not draw a line.
11. You and your partner take turns saying and writing words. Say a new word on the list each time.
12. Each time you draw a line, you are building a pen for the pig.
13. The object of this game is to be the person to draw the **last** line to make a square. This square is one pen. Put your initials in that pen. That pen is yours.
14. Watch the lines. Try to be the **last** person to draw the line to make a square.
15. When you and your partner have each written ten words, switch lists. Take turns saying and writing words again. Decide how many times you want to switch lists.
16. When you have finished switching lists, or when there are no more dots to use, the game is over.
17. Count the number of squares holding your initials.
18. The person with the most pens wins.

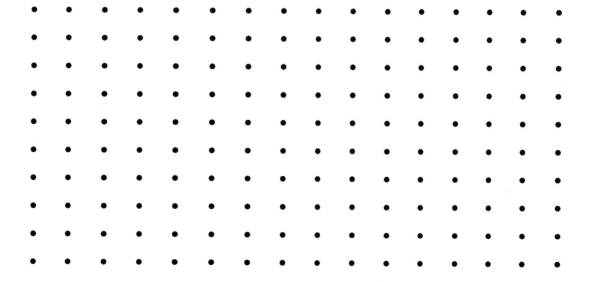

Backward Puzzle

Write a brief definition or clue for each word in the puzzle.

#	Word		#	Clue
1.	t o i l e t		1.	_____
2.	r u g		2.	_____
3.	c h a i r		3.	_____
4.	h o u s e		4.	_____
5.	c o u c h		5.	_____
	u			
6.	s i n k		6.	_____
7.	a p a r t m e n t		7.	_____
8.	k i t c h e n		8.	_____
9.	s t o v e		9.	_____
10.	c l o s e t		10.	_____
11.	v i d e o		11.	_____
12.	b a t h r o o m		12.	_____
13.	r e f r i g e r a t o r		13.	_____
14.	l i v i n g r o o m		14.	_____
15.	m i c r o w a v e		15.	_____
16.	b a t h t u b		16.	_____
17.	c a b l e		17.	_____
18.	b e d r o o m		18.	_____
19.	l a m p		19.	_____
20.	k e y		20.	_____

Find the hidden sentence that reads from the top down in the puzzle.
Write it here.

_____

Sneaky Snakes

Dissect (cut apart) these snakes by drawing lines through their bodies after every word. Write your starting, finishing, and total times for each snake. Try to do each snake faster than the last one.

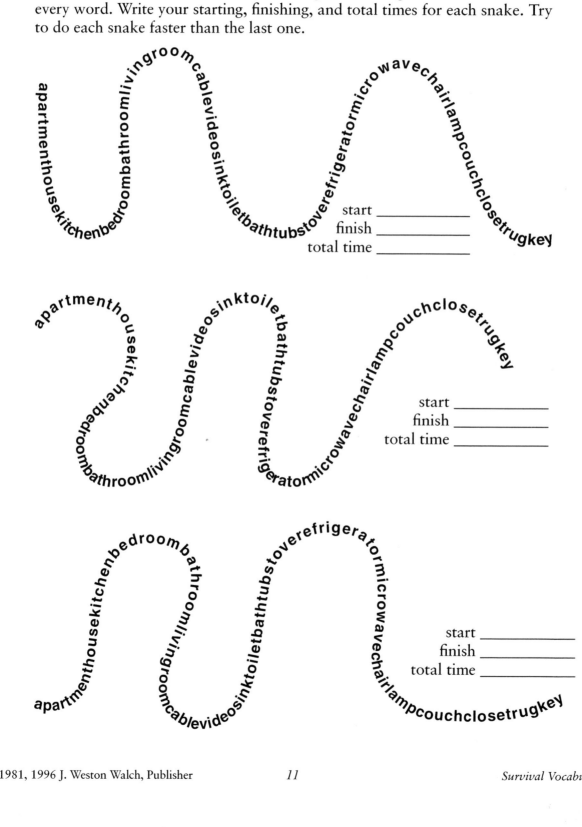

start _____

finish _____

total time _____

start _____

finish _____

total time _____

start _____

finish _____

total time _____

11

Survival Vocabulary

X-ray Vision

Write each word correctly.   **Write the words in alphabetical order.**

1. ahpahrtmint _____   _____

2. houss _____   _____

3. kitchun _____   _____

4. bedruum _____   _____

5. baathruum _____   _____

6. living ruum _____   _____

7. cabul _____   _____

8. vediyo _____   _____

9. singk _____   _____

10. toylett _____   _____

11. baathtub _____   _____

12. stov _____   _____

13. reefrijuratur _____   _____

14. mycroweve _____   _____

15. chayer _____   _____

16. laamp _____   _____

17. cowch _____   _____

18. clahzit _____   _____

19. rruugg _____   _____

20. kee _____   _____

Silly Dilly

Write a story using all of the following words. Make it interesting!

1. apartment	6. living room	11. bathtub	16. lamp
2. house	7. cable	12. stove	17. couch
3. kitchen	8. video	13. refrigerator	18. closet
4. bedroom	9. sink	14. microwave	19. rug
5. bathroom	10. toilet	15. chair	20. key

_____

_____

_____

_____

_____

_____

_____

_____

_____

_____

_____

_____

_____

_____

Unit 2
Food Words

tea

lunch

fruit

butter

bread

soup

eggs

fish

cookies

breakfast

vegetables

supper

juice

sugar

cereal

snack

milk

meat

coffee

soda

Survival Vocabulary

New Words and Lost Letters

Read each word and its definition. In the Lost Letters column, write each word by filling in the missing letters.

LOST LETTERS

1.	vegetables	plants that can be eaten	ve _ _ _ abl _ s
2.	fish	the flesh of an underwater animal used for food	f _ s _
3.	bread	a baked food made mainly of flour	_ _ ea _
4.	meat	animal tissue used for food	m _ _ _
5.	milk	a white liquid often used to feed babies	mi _ _
6.	soup	a liquid food with meat, fish, or vegetables as a base	_ _ _ p
7.	eggs	hard-shelled food produced by chickens	_ gg _
8.	butter	a solid food made by churning milk or cream	_ ut _ _ _
9.	coffee	a dark brown drink made from the beans of a particular tree	c _ _ _ e _
10.	soda	a sweet drink made of soda water and flavoring	s _ _ a
11.	tea	a drink made by pouring boiling water over dried leaves	t _ _
12.	fruit	part of a plant that has seeds and can be eaten	f _ _ _ t
13.	sugar	a white material taken from cane or beet and used to sweeten food	s _ g _ _
14.	breakfast	the first meal of the day	br _ _ k _ a _ _
15.	lunch	the second or noon meal of the day	_ _ n _ h
16.	supper	the last meal of the day	_ upp _ _
17.	cookies	small flat cakes	c _ _ _ _ _ s
18.	juice	the liquid of fruit and other foods	_ u _ c _
19.	snack	a small amount of food eaten between meals	_ na _ _
20.	cereal	a food made of grain	_ er _ al

Name _____

Date _____

Snoop and Solve

Find the words in the maze and circle them. The words may go across, up, down, or diagonally. Check them off in the list at the top as you find them.

___ 1. vegetables	___ 8. butter	___ 15. lunch
___ 2. fish	___ 9. coffee	___ 16. supper
___ 3. bread	___ 10. soda	___ 17. cookies
___ 4. meat	___ 11. tea	___ 18. juice
___ 5. milk	___ 12. fruit	___ 19. snack
___ 6. soup	___ 13. sugar	___ 20. cereal
___ 7. eggs	___ 14. breakfast	

v	w	a	t	e	w	r	t	s	s	m	s	u	c
e	e	t	b	o	t	a	r	e	u	s	i	t	o
g	e	g	r	s	e	o	t	s	a	g	i	l	o
t	f	s	e	m	s	e	e	e	s	u	a	s	k
d	f	o	a	t	j	u	i	c	r	d	s	m	i
b	o	b	k	b	a	e	s	f	e	e	u	e	e
l	c	a	f	d	r	b	r	o	p	s	h	g	s
e	s	n	a	c	k	e	l	e	p	s	c	g	b
m	m	e	s	o	e	r	a	e	u	e	n	m	u
i	r	i	t	o	e	r	n	k	s	o	u	p	t
b	r	x	l	t	d	u	e	e	f	u	l	s	e
l	q	o	t	l	l	a	b	a	g	a	g	b	r
a	j	u	i	c	e	e	d	b	l	g	s	a	r
b	b	c	e	r	f	i	s	h	e	r	t	m	r

17

Survival Vocabulary

Scrambled Eggs

Write the words correctly.   **Divide the words into syllables.**

1. vegtebales   _____   _____

2. shif   _____   _____

3. breda   _____   _____

4. eatm   _____   _____

5. mlki   _____   _____

6. ousp   _____   _____

7. gegs   _____   _____

8. tterbu   _____   _____

9. ffeeoc   _____   _____

10. ados   _____   _____

11. aet   _____   _____

12. uitrf   _____   _____

13. garsu   _____   _____

14. fastkearb   _____   _____

15. chlun   _____   _____

16. ppsuer   _____   _____

17. ooiesck   _____   _____

18. jucie   _____   _____

19. ckans   _____   _____

20. eeacrl   _____   _____

Survival Vocabulary

Pick a Pair

Write the number of each definition in front of the word it goes with.

____ vegetables	1. animal tissue used for food
____ fish	2. a sweet drink made of soda water and flavoring
____ bread	3. a small amount of food eaten between meals
____ meat	4. a solid food made by churning milk or cream
____ milk	5. the flesh of an underwater animal used for food
____ soup	6. the first meal of the day
____ eggs	7. part of a plant that has seeds and can be eaten
____ butter	8. a food made of grain
____ coffee	9. a white liquid often used to feed babies
____ soda	10. the last meal of the day
____ tea	11. small flat cakes
____ fruit	12. plants that can be eaten
____ sugar	13. the liquid of fruit and other foods
____ breakfast	14. a baked food made mainly of flour
____ lunch	15. the second or noon meal of the day
____ supper	16. a liquid food with meat, fish, or vegetables as a base
____ cookies	17. hard-shelled food produced by chickens
____ juice	18. a dark brown drink made from the beans of a particular tree
____ snack	19. a drink made by pouring boiling water over dried leaves
____ cereal	20. a white material taken from cane or beet and used to sweeten food

     Survival Vocabulary

Crack the Code

1 - a	6 - f	11 - k	16 - p	21 - u	24 - x
2 - b	7 - g	12 - l	17 - q	22 - v	25 - y
3 - c	8 - h	13 - m	18 - r	23 - w	26 - z
4 - d	9 - i	14 - n	19 - s		
5 - e	10 - j	15 - o	20 - t		

Write the letters under the numbers below to crack the code.

20 - 8 - 5 - 19 - 5 - 7 - 18 - 5 - 5 - 14 - 22 - 5 - 7 - 5 - 20 - 1 - 2 - 12 - 5 - 19 - 1 - 18 - 5 - 7 -

15 - 15 - 4 - 20 - 15 - 5 - 1 - 20.

12 - 5 - 20 - 19 - 5- 1- 20 - 19 - 21 - 16 - 16 - 5 - 18 - 20 - 15 - 7 - 5 - 20 - 8 - 5 - 18.

23 - 5 - 8 - 1 - 4 - 3 - 8 - 9 - 3 - 11 - 5 - 14 - 6 - 18 - 21 - 9 - 20 - 1 - 14 - 4 - 13 - 9 - 12 - 11 - 6 -

15 - 18 - 12 - 21 - 14 - 3 - 8.

2 - 18 - 5 - 1 - 11 - 6 - 1 - 19 - 20 - 3 - 1 - 14 - 2 - 5 - 10 - 21 - 9 - 3 - 5 - 3 - 5 - 18 - 5 - 1 - 12 -

1 - 14 - 4 - 13 - 9 - 12 - 11.

16 - 12 - 5 - 1 - 19 - 5 - 16 - 21 - 20 - 2 - 21 - 20 - 20 - 5 - 18 - 15 - 14 - 25 - 15 - 21 - 18 - 2 -

18 - 5 - 1 - 4.

23 - 5 - 8 - 1 - 4 - 20 - 8 - 18 - 5 - 5 - 3 - 15 - 15 - 11 - 9 - 5 - 19 - 6 - 15 - 18 - 1 - 19 - 14 - 1 -

3 - 11.

On the back of this page, write your own coded message. Ask your partner to crack it.

Sentence Sense

Read each sentence. One of the three sentences sounds correct. Circle the letter in front of the correct sentence.

1. (a) Stir a little white vegetables on your cereal.
   (b) I need a straw to drink these vegetables.
   (c) These vegetables must be washed before we eat them.

2. (a) This glass of fish is nice and cool.
   (b) Please spread some peanut butter on my fish.
   (c) I want to cut this fish into little pieces.

3. (a) Please pour me a cup of hot bread.
   (b) Please bread my dish with some vegetables.
   (c) I like this bread very much.

4. (a) He has a large piece of meat in his dish.
   (b) Please pour me a tall glass of meat.
   (c) He loves to drink meat with a straw.

5. (a) She cut her milk up into pieces.
   (b) My milk is nice and cold.
   (c) We picked up the pieces of milk.

6. (a) The soup I had for lunch was delicious.
   (b) The meal we had was no soup.
   (c) Please sprinkle some soup on my cereal.

7. (a) Please drink your eggs with a straw.
   (b) I put eggs in my tea to make it sweet.
   (c) My mother fixed me two eggs for breakfast.

8. (a) He drank a cool glass of butter.
   (b) She washed the butter before eating it.
   (c) The butter on my bread is soft.

9. (a) My father's coffee is too hot to drink.
   (b) Please pour this coffee on the soda.
   (c) She ate three cookies for coffee.

(continued)

Sentence Sense (continued)

10. (a) Her soda is in the soup.
    (b) I like orange soda.
    (c) Please cut the soda into larger pieces.

11. (a) I will eat this tea with my fork.
    (b) This tea is good to drink.
    (c) Please spread some tea on this bread.

12. (a) This fruit is good to eat after supper.
    (b) Our evening meal is at fruit time.
    (c) Let's go to fruit for the day.

13. (a) I drank that glass of sugar.
    (b) He has a little sugar in his tea.
    (c) Please sprinkle some bread on this sugar.

14. (a) My mother put some breakfast in his coffee.
    (b) Breakfast is an important meal of the day.
    (c) Please cut me a piece of breakfast.

15. (a) My sister will lunch the milk in her glass.
    (b) We ate a good lunch at noon.
    (c) We will have lunch before we get up this morning.

16. (a) Our family will eat supper this evening.
    (b) Please pour me a glass of supper.
    (c) Let's have supper this morning.

17. (a) My brother's cup of cookies is too hot to drink.
    (b) Please cookies my breakfast today.
    (c) These little brown cookies are very good.

18. (a) Please hand me a piece of juice.
    (b) This juice tastes so good at breakfast.
    (c) She will cut the juice into eight pieces.

19. (a) We eat a snack after school.
    (b) Snack is the first meal of the day.
    (c) Please snack my tea.

20. (a) The last meal of the day is cereal.
    (b) This cereal can be eaten at breakfast.
    (c) Please cut me a piece of meat for cereal.

Pen the Pig

1. Divide the list of words in Exercise 1 into two lists of ten words each.
2. Choose a partner. Give your partner one of the lists of ten words. You keep the other list.
3. Say one of the words on your list. Your partner writes it down on a sheet of paper.
4. You check your partner's spelling.
5. If the word is spelled correctly, your partner may touch his or her pencil to a dot and draw one straight line across or down to another dot.
6. If the word is not spelled correctly, your partner may not draw a line.
7. Now your partner says one of the words on his or her list to you. You write it down.
8. Your partner checks the spelling.
9. If the word is spelled correctly, you may draw one line between two dots, going across or down.
10. If the word is not spelled correctly, you may not draw a line.
11. You and your partner take turns saying and writing words. Say a new word on the list each time.
12. Each time you draw a line, you are building a pen for the pig.
13. The object of this game is to be the person to draw the **last** line to make a square. This square is one pen. Put your initials in that pen. That pen is yours.
14. Watch the lines. Try to be the **last** person to draw the line to make a square.
15. When you and your partner have each written ten words, switch lists. Take turns saying and writing words again. Decide how many times you want to switch lists.
16. When you have finished switching lists, or when there are no more dots to use, the game is over.
17. Count the number of squares holding your initials.
18. The person with the most pens wins.

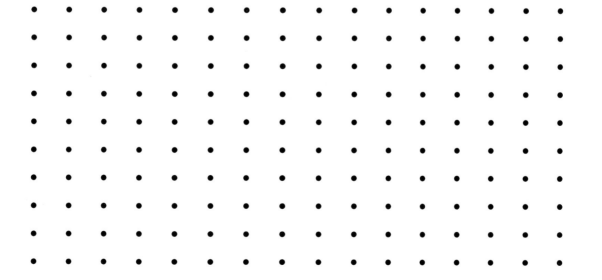

Name _____

Date _____

Backward Puzzle

Write a brief definition or clue for each word in the puzzle.

#	Puzzle		#	Answer
1.	b r e a k f a s t		1.	_____
2.	c e r e a l		2.	_____
3.	e g g s		3.	_____
4.	j u i c e		4.	_____
5.	b u t t e r		5.	_____
6.	v e g e t a b l e s		6.	_____
7.	t e a		7.	_____
8.	c o f f e e		8.	_____
9.	s u p p e r		9.	_____
10.	m e a t		10.	_____
11.	f r u i t		11.	_____
12.	s u g a r		12.	_____
13.	c o o k i e s		13.	_____
14.	s o u p		14.	_____
15.	s o d a		15.	_____
16.	m i l k		16.	_____
17.	b r e a d		17.	_____
18.	s n a c k		18.	_____
19.	l u n c h		19.	_____
20.	f i s h		20.	_____

Find the hidden sentence that reads from the top down in the puzzle.
Write it here.

_____

24   *Survival Vocabulary*

Sneaky Snakes

Dissect (cut apart) these snakes by drawing lines through their bodies after every word. Write your starting, finishing, and total times for each snake. Try to do each snake faster than the last one.

vegetablesfishbreadmeatmilksoupeggsbuttercoffeesodateafruitsugarbreakfastlunchsuppercookiesjuicesnackcereal

start _____
finish _____
total time _____

vegetablesfishbreadmeatmilksoupeggsbuttercoffeesodateafruitsugarbreakfastlunchsuppercookiesjuicesnackcereal

start _____
finish _____
total time _____

vegetablesfishbreadmeatmilksoupeggsbuttercoffeesodateafruitsugarbreakfastlunchsuppercookiesjuicesnackcereal

start _____
finish _____
total time _____

X-ray Vision

Write each word correctly.   **Write the words in alphabetical order.**

1. vehgtabuls   _____   _____

2. fisch   _____   _____

3. brehd   _____   _____

4. meet   _____   _____

5. millck   _____   _____

6. soop   _____   _____

7. egz   _____   _____

8. buttur   _____   _____

9. cawfee   _____   _____

10. sodah   _____   _____

11. tee   _____   _____

12. froot   _____   _____

13. shugur   _____   _____

14. breckfest   _____   _____

15. luunch   _____   _____

16. suhpur   _____   _____

17. cookeez   _____   _____

18. joos   _____   _____

19. snaak   _____   _____

20. ceereul   _____   _____

Silly Dilly

Write a story using all of the following words. Make it interesting!

1. vegetables
2. fish
3. bread
4. meat
5. milk

6. soup
7. eggs
8. butter
9. coffee
10. soda

11. tea
12. fruit
13. sugar
14. breakfast
15. lunch

16. supper
17. cookies
18. juice
19. snack
20. cereal

_____

_____

_____

_____

_____

_____

_____

_____

_____

_____

_____

_____

_____

cookies

Unit 3
Family Words

daughter   wife

grandfather   son

husband   sister

guardian   parents

aunt   uncle

mother   niece

nephew   stepfather

cousin   grandmother

brother   stepmother

children   father

New Words and Lost Letters

Read each word and its definition. In the Lost Letters column, write each word by filling in the missing letters.

LOST LETTERS

1.	mother	a woman who has borne a child	m _ _ _ er
2.	father	a male parent	_ _ th _ r
3.	sister	a woman or girl related to you by having the same parents	s _ _ _ _ r
4.	brother	a man or boy related to you by having the same parents	_ _ _ ther
5.	guardian	a person appointed to take care of another	g _ ar _ _ _ n
6.	children	sons and daughters in a family	c _ _ ld _ e _
7.	aunt	the sister of your father or mother	a _ _ _
8.	uncle	the brother of your father or mother	_ _ c _ _
9.	niece	the daughter of your sister or brother	_ _ _ ce
10.	nephew	the son of your sister or brother	_ _ _ _ ew
11.	cousin	the son or daughter of your uncle or aunt	_ _ _ _ in
12.	grandmother	the mother of your father or mother	_ _ _ _ _ mother
13.	grandfather	the father of your father or mother	_ rand _ _ _ _ _ r
14.	parents	a father and mother	_ _ re _ _ s
15.	wife	a woman to whom a man is married	_ if _
16.	husband	a man to whom a woman is married	hus _ _ _ d
17.	daughter	a person's female child	d _ _ g _ _ e _
18.	son	a person's male child	_ _ n
19.	stepmother	a woman married to your father after the death or divorce of your mother	_ _ _ _ mo _ _ _ r
20.	stepfather	a man married to your mother after the death or divorce of your father	_ te _ _ at _ _ _

Survival Vocabulary

Snoop and Solve

Find the words in the maze and circle them. The words may go across, up, down, or diagonally. Check them off in the list at the top as you find them.

___ 1. mother

___ 2. father

___ 3. sister

___ 4. brother

___ 5. guardian

___ 6. children

___ 7. aunt

___ 8. uncle

___ 9. niece

___ 10. nephew

___ 11. cousin

___ 12. grandmother

___ 13. grandfather

___ 14. parents

___ 15. wife

___ 16. husband

___ 17. daughter

___ 18. son

___ 19. stepmother

___ 20. stepfather

m	s	t	e	p	m	o	t	h	e	r	e	g	g
o	d	a	g	o	u	r	e	s	i	s	t	e	r
t	a	n	u	n	c	l	e	i	o	r	b	c	a
h	u	b	c	h	i	l	d	r	e	n	o	d	n
e	g	s	o	o	d	e	p	h	c	u	f	n	d
r	h	i	u	f	o	w	c	b	r	s	r	a	m
e	t	p	s	a	u	n	t	e	w	y	l	b	o
p	e	l	i	t	b	e	h	g	a	b	n	s	t
a	r	f	n	h	u	t	d	w	s	a	e	u	h
r	h	v	a	e	o	k	u	i	r	b	p	h	e
e	f	k	g	r	a	n	d	f	a	t	h	e	r
n	x	i	b	j	i	m	t	e	b	r	e	d	g
t	u	g	u	a	r	d	i	a	n	n	w	r	m
s	t	e	p	f	a	t	h	e	r	a	e	f	o

Scrambled Eggs

Write the words correctly.   **Divide the words into syllables.**

1. ermoth   _____   _____

2. athfre   _____   _____

3. ssteri   _____   _____

4. therorb   _____   _____

5. grainudan   _____   _____

6. ildrench   _____   _____

7. tnua   _____   _____

8. elunc   _____   _____

9. ience   _____   _____

10. hewpne   _____   _____

11. insouc   _____   _____

12. thermoandgr   _____   _____

13. rangdfaerth   _____   _____

14. rentpas   _____   _____

15. ifew   _____   _____

16. andhubs   _____   _____

17. terdaugh   _____   _____

18. ons   _____   _____

19. pestotherm   _____   _____

20. spetthefar   _____   _____

Pick a Pair

Write the number of each definition in front of the word it goes with.

_____ children

_____ grandmother

_____ mother

_____ son

_____ parents

_____ guardian

_____ wife

_____ father

_____ stepfather

_____ niece

_____ brother

_____ stepmother

_____ uncle

_____ sister

_____ husband

_____ aunt

_____ nephew

_____ cousin

_____ daughter

_____ grandfather

1. the daughter of your sister or brother

2. a father and mother

3. a male parent

4. a woman to whom a man is married

5. the father of your father or mother

6. the son or daughter of your uncle or aunt

7. a man married to your mother after the death or divorce of your father

8. a person appointed to take care of another

9. a woman who has borne a child

10. a person's male child

11. a man to whom a woman is married

12. the mother of your father or mother

13. the brother of your father or mother

14. sons and daughters in a family

15. a man or boy related to you by having the same parents

16. a woman married to your father after the death or divorce of your mother

17. a person's female child

18. the son of your sister or brother

19. the sister of your father or mother

20. a woman or girl related to you by having the same parents

Survival Vocabulary

Name _____

Date _____

Crack the Code

1 - a	6 - f	11 - k	16 - p	21 - u	24 - x
2 - b	7 - g	12 - l	17 - q	22 - v	25 - y
3 - c	8 - h	13 - m	18 - r	23 - w	26 - z
4 - d	9 - i	14 - n	19 - s		
5 - e	10 - j	15 - o	20 - t		

Write the letters under the numbers below to crack the code.

13 - 25 - 6 - 1 - 20 - 8 - 5 - 18 - 9 - 19 - 1 - 19 - 13 - 1 - 18 - 20 - 13 - 1 - 14.

20 - 8 - 15 - 19 - 5 - 3 - 8 - 9 - 12 - 4 - 18 - 5 - 14 - 1 - 18 - 5 - 16 - 12 - 1 - 25 - 9 - 14 - 7 - 2 - 1 - 12 - 12.

13 - 25 - 16 - 1 - 18 - 5 - 14 - 20 - 19 - 20 - 1 - 11 - 5 - 3 - 1 - 18 - 5 - 15 - 6 - 13 - 5.

25 - 15 - 21 - 18 - 19 - 9 - 19 - 20 - 5 - 18 - 11 - 14 - 15 - 23 - 19 - 13 - 25 - 2 - 18 - 15 - 20 - 8 - 5 - 18.

20 - 8 - 5 - 9 - 18 - 4 - 1 - 21 - 7 - 8 - 20 - 5 - 18 - 9 - 19 - 1 - 20 - 1 - 12 - 12 - 7 - 9 - 18 - 12.

13 - 25 - 1 - 21 - 14 - 20 - 1 - 14 - 4 - 21 - 14 - 3 - 12 - 5 - 12 - 9 - 22 - 5 - 23 - 9 - 20 - 8 - 21 - 19.

On the back of this page, write your own coded message here. Ask your partner to crack it.

Sentence Sense

Read each sentence. One of the three sentences sounds correct. Circle the letter in front of the correct sentence.

1. (a) My mother went to the store.
   (b) His mother is in the crib.
   (c) My mother is his grandfather.

2. (a) The child on the swing is his father.
   (b) Her father is at work.
   (c) We went to the father to eat supper.

3. (a) That girl is her sister.
   (b) Her sister is my uncle.
   (c) That dress is a beautiful sister.

4. (a) We read his brother at school.
   (b) We went home in his brother.
   (c) My brother is taller than my father.

5. (a) The baby is our guardian.
   (b) My guardian can drive us to the store.
   (c) Her brother will cook our guardian.

6. (a) All the children drive those big trucks to their jobs.
   (b) Those children are walking to school together.
   (c) Those little children will work with the machines.

7. (a) Her aunt is a very nice lady.
   (b) Let's go to the aunt to play and have fun.
   (c) My aunt is really her grandfather.

8. (a) Her uncle will work all day.
   (b) We found money at the uncle.
   (c) We can drive in the uncle to go to school.

9. (a) My niece is that little girl in the pink dress.
   (b) We found our hats and coats in the niece.
   (c) Her niece is my oldest brother.

(continued)

           Survival Vocabulary

Sentence Sense *(continued)*

10. (a) We ate breakfast in the nephew.
    (b) Her nephew is a young man.
    (c) Her sister is that boy's nephew.

11. (a) Your cousin can come with us to the beach.
    (b) Let's get in the cousin for a ride to school.
    (c) The yellow bus is the cousin we take to school.

12. (a) That man in the blue coat is my grandmother.
    (b) My grandmother makes bread for our family.
    (c) His brother will be my grandmother.

13. (a) My grandfather is my mother's father.
    (b) That tall woman is my friend's grandfather.
    (c) My aunt is really a very nice grandfather.

14. (a) Their parents is that short woman in the red dress.
    (b) Her parents are in the washer.
    (c) My parents take very good care of me.

15. (a) His wife is the man in the blue sweater.
    (b) The little boy is that man's wife.
    (c) My father's wife is my mother.

16. (a) Her husband is my sister.
    (b) Her husband is home from work.
    (c) Her husband is the mother of that little girl.

17. (a) That tall boy is my friend's daughter.
    (b) My son is my husband's daughter.
    (c) Their daughter is a very talented girl.

18. (a) That girl in the green coat is his son.
    (b) That man's son is my best friend.
    (c) The son of my uncle is a very short girl.

19. (a) Her stepmother will help us with the clothes.
    (b) That man near the door is my stepmother.
    (c) His stepmother is in that crib.

20. (a) Her stepfather is a very nice person.
    (b) My stepfather is a lovely woman.
    (c) Try to eat that stepfather in little bites.

Pen the Pig

1. Divide the list of words in Exercise 1 into two lists of ten words each.
2. Choose a partner. Give your partner one of the lists of ten words. You keep the other list.
3. Say one of the words on your list. Your partner writes it down on a sheet of paper.
4. You check your partner's spelling.
5. If the word is spelled correctly, your partner may touch his or her pencil to a dot and draw one straight line across or down to another dot.
6. If the word is not spelled correctly, your partner may not draw a line.
7. Now your partner says one of the words on his or her list to you. You write it down.
8. Your partner checks the spelling.
9. If the word is spelled correctly, you may draw one line between two dots, going across or down.
10. If the word is not spelled correctly, you may not draw a line.
11. You and your partner take turns saying and writing words. Say a new word on the list each time.
12. Each time you draw a line, you are building a pen for the pig.
13. The object of this game is to be the person to draw the **last** line to make a square. This square is one pen. Put your initials in that pen. That pen is yours.
14. Watch the lines. Try to be the **last** person to draw the line to make a square.
15. When you and your partner have each written ten words, switch lists. Take turns saying and writing words again. Decide how many times you want to switch lists.
16. When you have finished switching lists, or when there are no more dots to use, the game is over.
17. Count the number of squares holding your initials.
18. The person with the most pens wins.

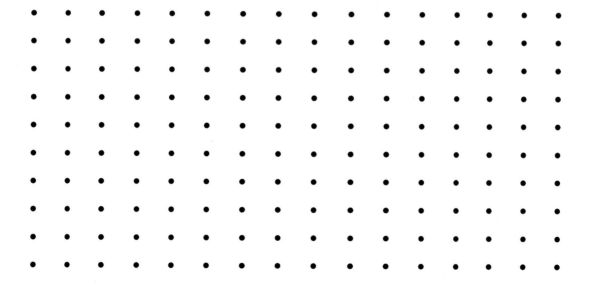

Backward Puzzle

Write a brief definition or clue for each word in the puzzle.

1. | m | o | t | h | e | r | | | |

2. | | | | d | a | u | g | h | t | e | r |

3. | | | u | n | c | l | e |

4. | | b | r | o | t | h | e | r |

5. | g | r | a | n | d | f | a | t | h | e | r |

6. | | | | a | u | n | t |

7. | | s | t | e | p | m | o | t | h | e | r |

8. | | | | n | i | e | c | e |

9. | | | c | h | i | l | d | r | e | n |

y

10. | g | u | a | r | d | i | a | n |

11. | | | | s | o | n |

12. | | g | r | a | n | d | m | o | t | h | e | r |

13. | | c | o | u | s | i | n |

14. | | | w | i | f | e |

15. | | s | t | e | p | f | a | t | h | e | r |

16. | | f | a | t | h | e | r |

17. | | | p | a | r | e | n | t | s |

18. | | n | e | p | h | e | w |

19. | h | u | s | b | a | n | d |

20. | | | s | i | s | t | e | r |

1. _____
2. _____
3. _____
4. _____
5. _____
6. _____
7. _____
8. _____
9. _____
10. _____
11. _____
12. _____
13. _____
14. _____
15. _____
16. _____
17. _____
18. _____
19. _____
20. _____

Find the hidden sentence that reads from the top down in the puzzle.
Write it here.

_____

Sneaky Snakes

Dissect (cut apart) these snakes by drawing lines through their bodies after every word. Write your starting, finishing, and total times for each snake. Try to do each snake faster than the last one.

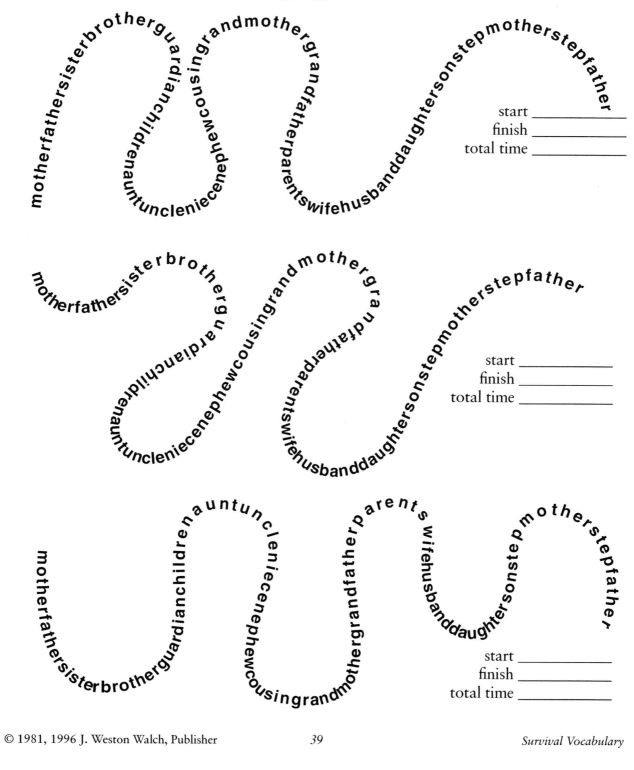

start _____
finish _____
total time _____

start _____
finish _____
total time _____

start _____
finish _____
total time _____

X-ray Vision

Write each word correctly.	**Write the words in alphabetical order.**

1. muthur _____ _____

2. fahthur _____ _____

3. sisstur _____ _____

4. bruthur _____ _____

5. gardien _____ _____

6. childrun _____ _____

7. ahnt _____ _____

8. uncul _____ _____

9. neec _____ _____

10. nefyou _____ _____

11. kuzyn _____ _____

12. grandmuthur _____ _____

13. grandfahthur _____ _____

14. pairunts _____ _____

15. wiif _____ _____

16. huzbund _____ _____

17. dawtur _____ _____

18. sun _____ _____

19. steppmuthur _____ _____

20. steppfahthur _____ _____

Survival Vocabulary

Silly Dilly

Write a story using all of the following words. Make it interesting!

1. mother	6. children	11. cousin	16. husband
2. father	7. aunt	12. grandmother	17. daughter
3. sister	8. uncle	13. grandfather	18. son
4. brother	9. niece	14. parents	19. stepmother
5. guardian	10. nephew	15. wife	20. stepfather

_____

_____

_____

_____

_____

_____

_____

_____

_____

_____

_____

_____

_____

_____

_____

Unit 4
Time Words

second

year

digital

month

day

calendar

hands

afternoon

watch

clock

P.M.

morning

week

hour

night

A.M.

date

noon

evening

minute

New Words and Lost Letters

Read each word and its definition. In the Lost Letters column, write each word by filling in the missing letters.

LOST LETTERS

1.	clock	an item for measuring time by means of pointers moving over a dial or by progressing numbers, usually not worn or carried by the user	_ _ ock
2.	watch	an item for measuring time, which is worn or carried by the user	w _ _ _ h
3.	hands	pointers on a clock	h _ _ ds
4.	digital	time shown in numbers	di _ _ t _ l
5.	calendar	a chart showing the days, weeks, and months of a year	_ _ _ _ _ da _
6.	day	a period of twenty-four hours, or the period of light between sunrise and sunset	d _ y
7.	week	seven days	_ _ _ k
8.	month	a period of four weeks or about thirty days	m _ _ t _
9.	year	twelve months	y _ _ _
10.	hour	one time unit—twenty-four of these units make one day	h _ _ r
11.	minute	one time unit—sixty of these units make one hour	_ _ _ u t _
12.	second	one time unit—sixty of these units make one minute	s _ _ _ _ d
13.	A.M.	before noon	_ . M.
14.	P.M.	after noon	P. _ .
15.	morning	the first part of the day from dawn to noon	_ _ _ ni _ _
16.	noon	the middle of the day at twelve o'clock	n _ _ n
17.	afternoon	the time from noon to evening	_ _ t _ rn _ _ _
18.	evening	the last part of the day and the early part of the night	_ _ _ _ i _ _
19.	night	the period of time from sunset to sunrise	n _ _ h _
20.	date	the time at which a thing happens	_ _ _ e

Snoop and Solve

Find the words in the maze and circle them. The words may go across, up, down, or diagonally. Check them off in the list at the top as you find them.

___ 1. clock	___ 8. month	___ 15. morning
___ 2. watch	___ 9. year	___ 16. noon
___ 3. hands	___ 10. hour	___ 17. afternoon
___ 4. digital	___ 11. minute	___ 18. evening
___ 5. calendar	___ 12. second	___ 19. night
___ 6. day	___ 13. A.M.	___ 20. date
___ 7. week	___ 14. P.M.	

s	e	v	e	n	i	n	g	c	c	d	i	s	r
u	c	c	b	u	a	k	e	r	y	l	l	u	e
p	b	a	t	m	b	d	s	n	l	q	o	s	h
e	a	a	l	b	n	k	o	t	e	h	a	c	c
A	s	m	e	e	e	o	y	a	t	r	t	r	k
M	k	i	o	r	n	r	o	n	k	a	e	e	t
r	e	n	k	r	r	d	o	n	w	c	e	p	h
m	e	u	e	m	n	m	a	c	l	w	e	i	n
l	s	t	r	o	l	i	c	r	e	r	P	M	g
y	f	e	c	p	t	s	n	k	y	h	c	a	e
a	m	e	e	k	h	t	e	g	e	e	n	t	e
d	s	s	d	i	g	i	t	a	l	a	a	o	m
o	t	h	a	l	i	l	b	a	s	d	o	r	t
r	u	b	h	a	n	d	s	k	e	e	s	r	a

Scrambled Eggs

Write the words correctly.   **Divide the words into syllables.**

 1. lccko   _____   _____

 2. hwatc   _____   _____

 3. anhds   _____   _____

 4. giltaid   _____   _____

 5. darencal   _____   _____

 6. ady   _____   _____

 7. ekew   _____   _____

 8. omnht   _____   _____

 9. reay   _____   _____

10. ouhr   _____   _____

11. utiemn   _____   _____

12. cesond   _____   _____

13. M.A.   _____   _____

14. M.P.   _____   _____

15. ingormn   _____   _____

16. nono   _____   _____

17. ternonoaf   _____   _____

18. eenvngi   _____   _____

19. inhgt   _____   _____

20. deta   _____   _____

Pick a Pair

Write the number of each definition in front of the word it goes with.

____ clock

____ watch

____ hands

____ digital

____ calendar

____ day

____ week

____ month

____ year

____ hour

____ minute

____ second

____ A.M.

____ P.M.

____ morning

____ noon

____ afternoon

____ evening

____ night

____ date

1. a period of four weeks or about thirty days

2. pointers on a clock

3. the time at which a thing happens

4. before noon

5. seven days

6. an item for measuring time by means of pointers moving over a dial or by progressing numbers, usually not worn or carried by the user

7. the period of time from sunset to sunrise

8. one time unit—sixty of these units make one hour

9. an item for measuring time, which is worn or carried by the user

10. after noon

11. the time from noon to evening

12. time shown in numbers

13. the last part of the day and the early part of the night

14. twelve months

15. one time unit—twenty-four of these units make one day

16. a chart showing the days, weeks, and months of a year

17. the middle of the day at twelve o'clock

18. a period of twenty-four hours, or the period of light between sunrise and sunset

19. the first part of the day from dawn to noon

20. one time unit—sixty of these units make one minute

       Survival Vocabulary

Crack the Code

1 - a	7 - g	12 - l	17 - q	22 - v
2 - b	8 - h	13 - m	18 - r	23 - w
3 - c	9 - i	14 - n	19 - s	24 - x
4 - d	10 - j	15 - o	20 - t	25 - y
5 - e	11 - k	16 - p	21 - u	26 - z
6 - f				

Write the letters under the numbers below to crack the code.

9 - 23 - 5 - 1 - 18 - 13 - 25 - 23 - 1 - 20 - 3 - 8 - 15 - 14 - 13 - 25 - 23 - 18 - 9 - 19 - 20.

12 - 15 - 15 - 11 - 1 - 20 - 20 - 8 - 5 - 3 - 12 - 15 - 3 - 11 - 20 - 15 - 19 - 5 - 5 - 20 - 8 - 5 - 20 -

9 - 13 - 5.

23 - 5 - 8 - 1 - 22 - 5 - 2 - 18 - 5 - 1 - 11 - 6 - 1 - 19 - 20 - 9 - 14 - 20 - 8 - 5 - 13 - 15 - 18 - 14 -

9 - 14 - 7.

15 - 21 - 18 - 3 - 15 - 13 - 16 - 1 - 14 - 25 - 3 - 1 - 13 - 5 - 20 - 15 - 19 - 21 - 16 - 16 - 5 - 18.

20 - 8 - 5 - 3 - 1 - 12 - 5 - 14 - 4 - 1 - 18 - 8 - 1 - 14 - 7 - 19 - 15 - 14 - 20 - 8 - 5 - 23 - 1 - 12 -

12.

23 - 5 - 23 - 1 - 20 - 3 - 8 - 20 - 22 - 9 - 14 - 20 - 8 - 5 - 5 - 22 - 5 - 14 - 9 - 14 - 7.

On another sheet of paper, write your own coded message. Ask your partner to crack it.

             Survival Vocabulary

Sentence Sense

Read each sentence. One of the three sentences sounds correct. Circle the letter in front of the correct sentence.

1. (a) She isn't wearing her clock today because it's broken.
   (b) We need a clock in our room to be able to see the time.
   (c) My mother gets up very early in the clock.

2. (a) The watch my sister is wearing is a gift from our family.
   (b) Please help me hang this large watch on the wall of the kitchen.
   (c) The watch today is written on my notebook cover.

3. (a) The hands in one hour are sixty minutes.
   (b) The hands on my grandfather's clock are bent and broken.
   (c) Let's write the hands of the holidays in our book.

4. (a) The numbers on a digital clock show the exact time.
   (b) The digital meal is eaten at the middle part of the day.
   (c) He can hang that large digital on the wall in our bedroom.

5. (a) Please wear your calendar on your left wrist.
   (b) The calendar will tell us the time of day we should eat supper.
   (c) We look at a calendar to see the days, weeks, and months.

6. (a) This day is very bright and sunny.
   (b) Please write down the day of when school starts.
   (c) This day is really four months on the calendar.

7. (a) The week she's wearing is so beautiful.
   (b) There are seven days in one week.
   (c) A week is the period of light from sunrise to sunset.

8. (a) This month is one time unit of one minute.
   (b) We can do many projects during the weeks in this month.
   (c) My brother put that month on the table in our bedroom.

9. (a) We can see the movie at seven o'clock in the year tonight.
   (b) We had many good times at school this year.
   (c) This year has only four weeks in it.

(continued)

Sentence Sense (continued)

10. (a) We will work on language during the next hour of this day.
    (b) Please turn the page of the hour to see the date of that holiday.
    (c) That hour is too big to fit on that little table.

11. (a) Please wait one minute while I sign your pass to the nurse.
    (b) Next minute we can go swimming when it's warm.
    (c) We always eat our minute together in the morning.

12. (a) The second on the clock points to the numbers.
    (b) One second is such a tiny unit of time.
    (c) One second has seven days in it.

13. (a) School begins at nine A.M. on five days of the week.
    (b) Please write the A.M. of her birthday on the calendar.
    (c) My A.M. is not working correctly today.

14. (a) We always eat breakfast at ten P.M. in the morning.
    (b) The P.M. on that clock shows how many minutes are in an hour.
    (c) Our family likes to eat supper about five P.M. each day.

15. (a) The morning is the last part of the day just before night.
    (b) The birds sing the loudest very early in the morning.
    (c) Every morning always lasts twelve months.

16. (a) The noon on this clock says it's eight o'clock.
    (b) Noon is always at twelve o'clock in the middle of the day.
    (c) Noon is the period of light between sunrise and sunset.

17. (a) We can go skating tomorrow afternoon after we eat lunch.
    (b) This afternoon had four very busy weeks.
    (c) Her father works every afternoon from nine A.M. until noon.

18. (a) I always eat my breakfast in the evening with my sister.
    (b) Each evening after supper, our family visits with my aunt.
    (c) The evening is only one unit of sixty units in one day.

19. (a) Please write the night in my notebook.
    (b) We can go to the library at night after we eat our supper.
    (c) A date is always sixty units making up one minute.

20. (a) The date of that holiday is written on the chalkboard.
    (b) He told her to come for a checkup next date on the fifth.
    (c) A date is always sixty units making up one minute.

Pen the Pig

1. Divide the list of words in Exercise 1 into two lists of ten words each.
2. Choose a partner. Give your partner one of the lists of ten words. You keep the other list.
3. Say one of the words on your list. Your partner writes it down on a sheet of paper.
4. You check your partner's spelling.
5. If the word is spelled correctly, your partner may touch his or her pencil to a dot and draw one straight line across or down to another dot.
6. If the word is not spelled correctly, your partner may not draw a line.
7. Now your partner says one of the words on his or her list to you. You write it down.
8. Your partner checks the spelling.
9. If the word is spelled correctly, you may draw one line between two dots, going across or down.
10. If the word is not spelled correctly, you may not draw a line.

11. You and your partner take turns saying and writing words. Say a new word on the list each time.
12. Each time you draw a line, you are building a pen for the pig.
13. The object of this game is to be the person to draw the **last** line to make a square. This square is one pen. Put your initials in that pen. That pen is yours.
14. Watch the lines. Try to be the **last** person to draw the line to make a square.
15. When you and your partner have each written ten words, switch lists. Take turns saying and writing words again. Decide how many times you want to switch lists.
16. When you have finished switching lists, or when there are no more dots to use, the game is over.
17. Count the number of squares holding your initials.
18. The person with the most pens wins.

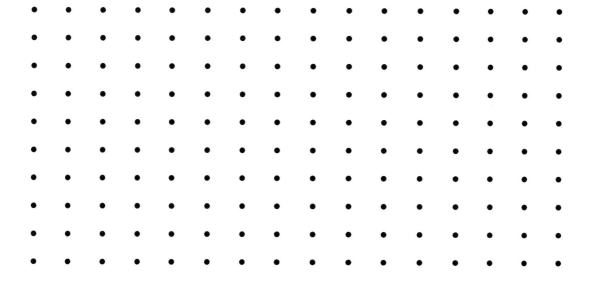

Backward Puzzle

Write a brief definition or clue for each word in the puzzle.

#	Puzzle	#	Clue
1.	d i g i t a l	1.	_____
2.	n i g h t	2.	_____
3.	a m	3.	_____
4.	w e e k	4.	_____
5.	m o n t h	5.	_____
6.	e v e n i n g	6.	_____
7.	c l o c k	7.	_____
8.	p m	8.	_____
9.	h a n d s	9.	_____
10.	h o u r	10.	_____
11.	s e c o n d	11.	_____
	p		
12.	c a l e n d a r	12.	_____
13.	w a t c h	13.	_____
14.	m o r n i n g	14.	_____
15.	n o o n	15.	_____
16.	m i n u t e	16.	_____
17.	a f t e r n o o n	17.	_____
18.	d a y	18.	_____
19.	d a t e	19.	_____
20.	y e a r	20.	_____

Find the hidden sentence that reads from the top down in the puzzle.
Write it here.

_____

       Survival Vocabulary

Sneaky Snakes

Dissect (cut apart) these snakes by drawing lines through their bodies after every word. Write your starting, finishing, and total times for each snake. Try to do each snake faster than the last one.

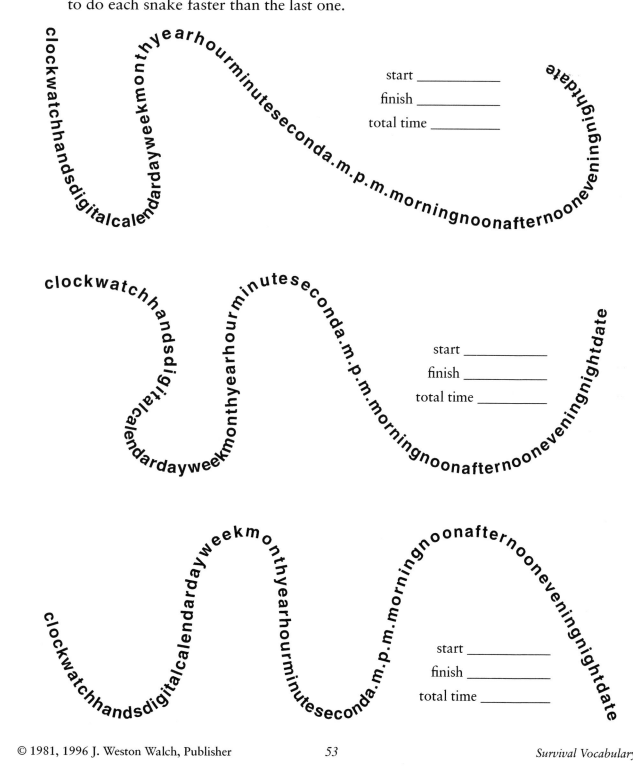

start _____

finish _____

total time _____

start _____

finish _____

total time _____

start _____

finish _____

total time _____

X-ray Vision

Write each word correctly.   **Write the words in alphabetical order.**

1. clahk   _____   _____

2. wawch   _____   _____

3. hanz   _____   _____

4. digetle   _____   _____

5. calindur   _____   _____

6. daaee   _____   _____

7. weeeck   _____   _____

8. munth   _____   _____

9. yeeeur   _____   _____

10. owurr   _____   _____

11. minitt   _____   _____

12. sekunt   _____   _____

13. aay emm   _____   _____

14. pee emm   _____   _____

15. mornning   _____   _____

16. nuun   _____   _____

17. afturnuun   _____   _____

18. eevning   _____   _____

19. niit   _____   _____

20. daaat   _____   _____

Silly Dilly

Write a story using all of the following words. Make it interesting!

1. clock	6. day	11. minute	16. noon
2. watch	7. week	12. second	17. afternoon
3. hands	8. month	13. A.M.	18. evening
4. digital	9. year	14. P.M.	19. night
5. calendar	10. hour	15. morning	20. date

_____

_____

_____

_____

_____

_____

_____

_____

_____

_____

_____

_____

_____

_____

_____

_____

_____

Unit 5
Food Store Words

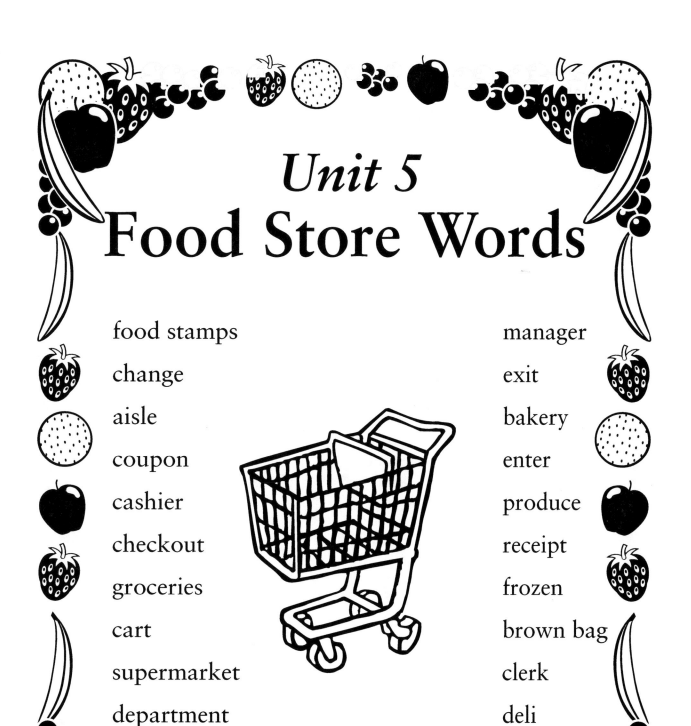

food stamps

change

aisle

coupon

cashier

checkout

groceries

cart

supermarket

department

manager

exit

bakery

enter

produce

receipt

frozen

brown bag

clerk

deli

Survival Vocabulary

New Words and Lost Letters

Read each word and its definition. In the Lost Letters column, write each word by filling in the missing letters.

LOST LETTERS

1.	supermarket	a large store selling food and other goods	_ _ per_ _ _ ket
2.	groceries	food and household items	_ _ oc_ rie_
3.	cart	a container used to carry groceries	_ a _ t
4.	checkout	a counter where groceries are paid for	c_ _ ck _ _ t
5.	cashier	a person in charge of money	_ _ sh _ _ _
6.	coupon	a ticket used to get money off the price of an item	co_ _ _ n
7.	produce	crops grown by a farmer	p_ _ du _ e
8.	bakery	a place where bread and pastries are sold	_ _ k _ ry
9.	department	a section of a store	_ _ par _ _ _ nt
10.	frozen	as cold and as hard as ice	_ _ _ z _ n
11.	aisle	a walkway between rows of stacked items	a _ _ l _
12.	manager	a person in charge	m _ n _ g _ _
13.	clerk	a person who sells in a store	cl _ _ _
14.	food stamps	paper issued to people for use as cash to buy food	f _ o _ st _ _ _ _
15.	brown bag	a paper holder in which to put groceries and other items	b _ _ wn b _ g
16.	enter	to go in or come in	_ nt _ _
17.	exit	a way out	_ x _ t
18.	deli	a place where prepared and cooked foods are sold	d _ _ _
19.	receipt	a slip of paper marked with the amount paid	re _ _ _ _ t
20.	change	money owed to a buyer who pays more than is due	ch _ _ _ _

Survival Vocabulary

Snoop and Solve

Find the words in the maze and circle them. The words may go across, up, down, or diagonally. Check them off in the list at the top as you find them.

___ 1. supermarket   ___ 8. bakery   ___ 15. brown bag

___ 2. groceries   ___ 9. department   ___ 16. enter

___ 3. cart   ___ 10. frozen   ___ 17. exit

___ 4. checkout   ___ 11. aisle   ___ 18. deli

___ 5. cashier   ___ 12. manager   ___ 19. receipt

___ 6. coupon   ___ 13. clerk   ___ 20. change

___ 7. produce   ___ 14. food stamps

t	r	a	c	k	e	t	k	f	r	o	f	z	s
g	b	y	p	r	e	r	w	r	o	d	r	e	u
a	r	a	e	t	e	k	g	e	u	e	o	n	p
b	e	o	i	l	b	a	a	g	t	o	z	o	e
d	r	x	c	k	o	r	b	n	u	o	e	p	r
e	e	a	r	e	e	c	e	a	o	i	n	u	m
p	l	b	f	g	r	a	e	h	k	l	o	o	a
a	s	d	a	y	m	i	e	c	c	e	m	c	r
r	i	n	k	s	k	c	e	k	e	d	r	e	k
t	a	b	e	k	u	b	a	s	h	l	m	y	e
m	t	a	r	d	e	t	r	e	c	e	i	p	t
e	h	c	o	f	o	o	d	s	t	a	m	p	s
n	e	r	s	b	r	o	w	n	b	a	g	t	t
t	p	f	r	o	z	c	a	s	h	i	e	r	o

Scrambled Eggs

Write the words correctly.   **Divide the words into syllables.**

1. supmareket   _____   _____

2. cergroies   _____   _____

3. trac   _____   _____

4. eckchotu   _____   _____

5. shrieac   _____   _____

6. puocno   _____   _____

7. ucedpro   _____   _____

8. erybak   _____   _____

9. mtnetrapde   _____   _____

10. zoenfr   _____   _____

11. saile   _____   _____

12. aaergmn   _____   _____

13. eclkr   _____   _____

14. dofo mpatss   _____   _____

15. bnowr gba   _____   _____

16. treen   _____   _____

17. tixe   _____   _____

18. lide   _____   _____

19. eeicrpt   _____   _____

20. aenghc   _____   _____

Pick a Pair

Write the number of each definition in front of the word it goes with.

____ supermarket

____ groceries

____ cart

____ checkout

____ cashier

____ coupon

____ produce

____ bakery

____ department

____ frozen

____ aisle

____ manager

____ clerk

____ food stamps

____ brown bag

____ enter

____ exit

____ deli

____ receipt

____ change

1. a counter where groceries are paid for

2. a person in charge

3. a section of a store

4. a walkway between rows of stacked items

5. to go in or come in

6. crops grown by a farmer

7. a slip of paper marked with the amount paid

8. a large store selling food and other goods

9. paper issued to people for use as cash to buy food

10. food and household items

11. as cold and as hard as ice

12. money owed to a buyer who pays more than is due

13. a way out

14. a place where prepared and cooked foods are sold

15. a container used to carry groceries

16. a ticket used to get money off the price of an item

17. a paper holder in which to put groceries and other items

18. a person in charge of money

19. a place where bread and pastries are sold

20. a person who sells in a store

Crack the Code

1 - a	7 - g	12 - l	17 - q	22 - v
2 - b	8 - h	13 - m	18 - r	23 - w
3 - c	9 - i	14 - n	19 - s	24 - x
4 - d	10 - j	15 - o	19 - s	25 - y
5 - e	11 - k	16 - p	20 - t	26 - z
6 - f			21 - u	

Write the letters under the numbers below to crack the code.

12 - 5 - 20 - 19 - 19 - 8 - 15 - 16 - 6 - 15 - 18 - 7 - 18 - 15 - 3 - 5 - 18 - 9 - 5 - 19.

20 - 8 - 5 - 3 - 1 - 19 - 8 - 9 - 5 - 18 - 23 - 9 - 12 - 12 - 20 - 1 - 11 - 5 - 15 - 21 - 18 - 13 - 15 - 14 - 5 - 25.

16 - 21 - 20 - 20 - 8 - 5 - 6 - 18 - 15 - 26 - 5 - 14 - 6 - 15 - 15 - 4 - 4 - 15 - 23 - 14.

20 - 8 - 5 - 2 - 1 - 11 - 5 - 18 - 25 - 9 - 19 - 15 - 14 - 20 - 8 - 9 - 19 - 1 - 9 - 19 - 12 - 5.

23 - 5 - 14 - 5 - 5 - 4 - 1 - 2 - 18 - 15 - 23 - 14 - 2 - 1 - 7 - 6 - 15 - 18 - 20 - 8 - 5 - 16 - 18 - 15 - 4 - 21 - 3 - 5.

8 - 5 - 2 - 15 - 21 - 7 - 8 - 20 - 13 - 5 - 1 - 20 - 1 - 20 - 20 - 8 - 5 - 4 - 5 - 12 - 9.

Write your own coded message here. Ask your partner to crack it.

Sentence Sense

Read each sentence. One of the three sentences sounds correct. Circle the letter in front of the correct sentence.

1. (a) The supermarket near our house has many kinds of food.
   (b) Please help me bring the supermarket to the checkout.
   (c) Ask her for a supermarket to prove that we paid the bill.

2. (a) Please get some big groceries to put this food in.
   (b) Please tear off these groceries from the paper so we can use them.
   (c) We have so many groceries to carry home this week.

3. (a) We need a shopping cart to push along the aisle for the groceries.
   (b) Make sure you count the cart the cashier gave you.
   (c) That cart is where we can buy the fresh bread.

4. (a) I can always buy cooked meat at the checkout by the door.
   (b) The checkout is near the door in the big supermarket.
   (c) Please help me put these big bottles in this brown checkout.

5. (a) Always count the change the cashier gives you back.
   (b) The cashier is the place where we can buy fresh produce.
   (c) There's a large cashier on the corner of our street.

6. (a) Let's walk down this coupon to find the canned fruit.
   (b) Please give the coupon to the cashier before she totals the cost of the food.
   (c) My sister ate the coupon she bought at the store.

7. (a) He cut all the produce out of the newspaper this week.
   (b) The produce in this department always looks fresh.
   (c) That lady gave us food produce to use as money to buy food.

8. (a) I love to buy pastries at this bakery to take home.
   (b) We can fit all these groceries in one bakery.
   (c) Please pick up a bakery at the door when you enter.

9. (a) Please ask her what department has the crackers and cookies.
   (b) That man will count our food and take our money at the department.
   (c) We can always buy prepared department at the deli counter.

(continued)

Sentence Sense *(continued)*

10. (a) I need to get a frozen to put all these groceries in.
    (b) It's hard to carry frozen food because it's so cold.
    (c) We can walk down this frozen to get to the meat department.

11. (a) Make sure you take an aisle when you come into the store.
    (b) This aisle sells delicious potato salad.
    (c) The eggs and butter are down this aisle.

12. (a) We need to talk to the manager of the store about a job.
    (b) I usually push a manager in this store because I buy a lot.
    (c) The manager can be found in most of our newspapers.

13. (a) Let's ask the clerk where the tissues are.
    (b) I always clerk the girl enough money to pay for everything.
    (c) I think the canned vegetables are down this clerk.

14. (a) We can ask food stamps to count our groceries and bill us.
    (b) These food stamps will help us buy our milk and rolls.
    (c) I need two food stamps to carry all these groceries home in.

15. (a) I hope this brown bag won't break with all these bottles in it.
    (b) We can use this brown bag to push down the aisle as we choose our food.
    (c) Please help me find the brown bag where the meat is sold.

16. (a) She forgot to give me my enter after I paid her.
    (b) These groceries are too heavy to enter home.
    (c) Let's enter the supermarket here.

17. (a) Let's try to fit as much food as we can in this exit.
    (b) My exit says I'm number six to be waited on.
    (c) I can push the cart out through this exit.

18. (a) I cut several deli out of the paper to use as cash.
    (b) The chicken at this deli is all cooked and ready to eat.
    (c) I forgot to take a deli as I came in.

19. (a) Be sure to keep the receipt the cashier gave you.
    (b) The receipt I buy in this store always tastes delicious.
    (c) I don't know how much receipt I should get back as change.

20. (a) We need lots of change to carry these groceries in.
    (b) I always count the cashier after I give her the change.
    (c) That cashier gave me the correct change.

Pen the Pig

1. Divide the list of words in Exercise 1 into two lists of ten words each.
2. Choose a partner. Give your partner one of the lists of ten words. You keep the other list.
3. Say one of the words on your list. Your partner writes it down on a sheet of paper.
4. You check your partner's spelling.
5. If the word is spelled correctly, your partner may touch his or her pencil to a dot and draw one straight line across or down to another dot.
6. If the word is not spelled correctly, your partner may not draw a line.
7. Now your partner says one of the words on his or her list to you. You write it down.
8. Your partner checks the spelling.
9. If the word is spelled correctly, you may draw one line between two dots, going across or down.
10. If the word is not spelled correctly, you may not draw a line.
11. You and your partner take turns saying and writing words. Say a new word on the list each time.
12. Each time you draw a line, you are building a pen for the pig.
13. The object of this game is to be the person to draw the **last** line to make a square. This square is one pen. Put your initials in that pen. That pen is yours.
14. Watch the lines. Try to be the **last** person to draw the line to make a square.
15. When you and your partner have each written ten words, switch lists. Take turns saying and writing words again. Decide how many times you want to switch lists.
16. When you have finished switching lists, or when there are no more dots to use, the game is over.
17. Count the number of squares holding your initials.
18. The person with the most pens wins.

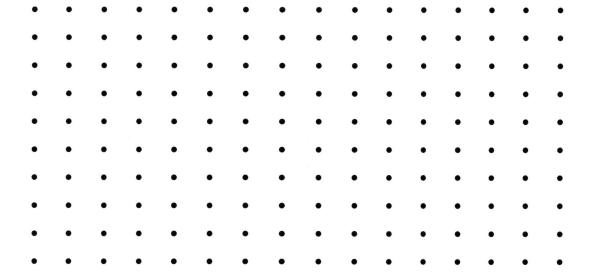

Backward Puzzle

Write a brief definition or clue for each word in the puzzle.

#	Word		#	
1.	brownbag		1.	_____
2.	enter		2.	_____
3.	clerk		3.	_____
4.	exit		4.	_____
5.	bakery		5.	_____
6.	supermarket		6.	_____
7.	aisle		7.	_____
8.	cashier		8.	_____
9.	coupon		9.	_____
10.	produce		10.	_____
11.	department		11.	_____
12.	receipt		12.	_____
13.	change		13.	_____
14.	manager		14.	_____
	f			
15.	checkout		15.	_____
16.	cart		16.	_____
17.	frozen		17.	_____
18.	groceries		18.	_____
19.	foodstamps		19.	_____
20.	deli		20.	_____

Find the hidden sentence that reads from the top down in the puzzle.
Write it here.

_____

Sneaky Snakes

Dissect (cut apart) these snakes by drawing lines through their bodies after every word. Write your starting, finishing, and total times for each snake. Try to do each snake faster than the last one.

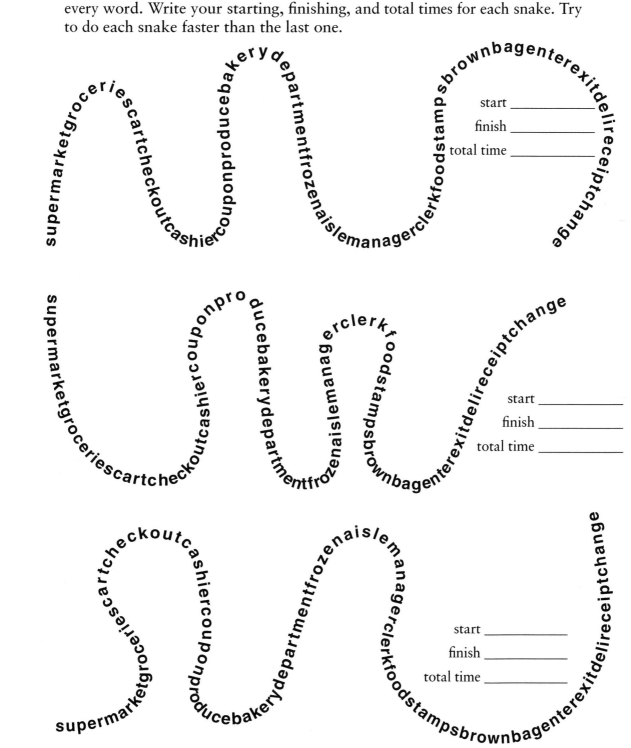

start _____

finish _____

total time _____

start _____

finish _____

total time _____

start _____

finish _____

total time _____

X-ray Vision

Write each word correctly.   **Write the words in alphabetical order.**

1. sooprmarkit   _____   _____

2. grocreez   _____   _____

3. cawrt   _____   _____

4. chekowt   _____   _____

5. casheeer   _____   _____

6. cupon   _____   _____

7. prohdoos   _____   _____

8. baykereee   _____   _____

9. deepahrtmint   _____   _____

10. furosin   _____   _____

11. iilll   _____   _____

12. manahjur   _____   _____

13. clurk   _____   _____

14. fhud staamppz   _____   _____

15. braun bagg   _____   _____

16. enntur   _____   _____

17. eggzit   _____   _____

18. delee   _____   _____

19. reeseet   _____   _____

20. chainj   _____   _____

Silly Dilly

Write a story using all of the following words. Make it interesting!

1. supermarket
2. groceries
3. cart
4. checkout
5. cashier

6. coupon
7. produce
8. bakery
9. department
10. frozen

11. aisle
12. manager
13. clerk
14. food stamps
15. brown bag

16. enter
17. exit
18. deli
19. receipt
20. change

_____

_____

_____

_____

_____

_____

_____

_____

_____

_____

_____

_____

_____

_____

_____

_____

_____

_____

Unit 6
School Words

computer	board	paper
microchip	teacher	pencil
auditorium	chalk	bell
principal	fire drill	software
gym	period	class
desk	office	Internet
cafeteria		homework

New Words and Lost Letters

Read each word and its definition. In the Lost Letters column, write each word by filling in the missing letters.

LOST LETTERS

1.	class	a group of students taught together	c _ _ _ s
2.	teacher	a person who gives instruction or shows how to do something	t _ _ c _ _ r
3.	period	a portion of time; also, a dot at the end of a sentence	pe _ _ _ d
4.	auditorium	a large room where groups of people can meet	_ _ d _ t _ r _ um
5.	cafeteria	a large dining area where people buy food at a counter and carry it to a table to eat	ca _ _ t _ r _ _
6.	fire drill	practice leaving the building in case of fire	f _ r _ _ ri _ l
7.	computer	a machine that processes and stores information	_ om_ u_ e_
8.	desk	a piece of furniture with a flat top on which to write	d _ _ _
9.	pencil	a pointed tool to write with	pen _ _ _
10.	paper	a thin sheet used for writing or printing	pa _ _ er
11.	office	a place where most of the paperwork is done for a school or a business	off _ _ e
12.	principal	the head person in a school	p _ _ _ _ _ p _ _
13.	Internet	a huge computer network where information can be found and shared	_ _ te _ ne _
14.	bell	something that makes a ringing sound	b _ _ _
15.	software	the program or instructions that tell a computer what to do	_ o _ tw _ _ e
16.	gym	a large room for games and exercise; also, physical education class	_ y _
17.	microchip	a tiny square of thin material used in electronic equipment	m _ c _ oc _ i _
18.	board	a flat, dark surface for writing on with chalk	boa _ _
19.	chalk	soft, white limestone used to write with	_ _ _ _ k
20.	homework	schoolwork done at home	h _ _ _ w _ _ _

Survival Vocabulary

Name _____

Date _____

Snoop and Solve

Find the words in the maze and circle them. The words may go across, up, down, or diagonally. Check them off in the list at the top as you find them.

____ 1. class	____ 8. desk	____ 15. software
____ 2. teacher	____ 9. pencil	____ 16. gym
____ 3. period	____ 10. paper	____ 17. microchip
____ 4. auditorium	____ 11. office	____ 18. board
____ 5. cafeteria	____ 12. principal	____ 19. chalk
____ 6. fire drill	____ 13. Internet	____ 20. homework
____ 7. computer	____ 14. bell	

h	o	m	e	w	o	r	k	p	p	a	p	e	r
s	u	c	h	a	l	k	s	i	r	i	n	l	e
g	o	n	e	h	o	c	e	h	i	m	m	l	o
g	y	f	c	w	h	h	d	c	u	r	c	e	o
l	y	o	t	e	k	r	g	o	m	l	o	b	l
l	b	m	f	w	r	f	e	r	i	g	m	a	m
i	o	c	t	d	a	s	r	c	e	d	p	i	i
r	a	l	e	o	s	r	n	i	e	i	u	r	r
d	r	a	n	i	f	e	e	m	c	s	t	e	e
e	d	s	r	r	p	f	c	n	i	o	e	t	h
r	n	s	e	e	k	a	i	f	l	s	r	e	c
i	i	a	t	p	e	r	f	c	d	d	i	f	a
f	o	j	n	t	p	o	m	l	e	l	d	a	e
a	u	d	i	t	o	r	i	u	m	c	k	c	t

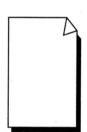

Scrambled Eggs

Write the words correctly.   **Divide the words into syllables.**

1. lassc _____   _____

2. cheeart _____   _____

3. rioped _____   _____

4. doraitumiu _____   _____

5. faireetac _____   _____

6. iref lidrl _____   _____

7. percumot _____   _____

8. eksd _____   _____

9. cilnep _____   _____

10. repap _____   _____

11. eicfof _____   _____

12. ciinarppl _____   _____

13. tintreen _____   _____

14. lebl _____   _____

15. fatersow _____   _____

16. ymg _____   _____

17. ciphomirc _____   _____

18. drboa _____   _____

19. kahlc _____   _____

20. ooerwmkh _____   _____

Pick a Pair

Write the number of each definition in front of the word it goes with.

____ class

1. a place where most of the paperwork is done for a school or a business

____ teacher

2. a machine that processes and stores information

____ period

3. a group of students taught together

____ auditorium

4. soft white limestone used to write with

____ cafeteria

5. a pointed tool to write with

____ fire drill

6. schoolwork done at home

____ computer

7. a portion of time; also, a dot at the end of a sentence

____ desk

8. a large room for games, and exercise; also, physical education class

____ pencil

9. a person who gives instruction or shows how to do something

____ paper

10. practice leaving the building in case of fire

____ office

11. a flat dark surface for writing on with chalk

____ principal

12. a huge computer network where information can be found and shared

____ Internet

13. the head person in a school

____ bell

14. a large room where groups of people can meet

____ software

15. a tiny square of thin material used in electronic equipment

____ gym

16. the program or instructions that tell a computer what to do

____ microchip

17. a piece of furniture with a flat top on which to write

____ board

18. something that makes a ringing sound

____ chalk

19. a thin sheet used for writing or printing

____ homework

20. a large dining area where people buy food at a counter and carry it to a table to eat

Survival Vocabulary

Crack the Code

1 - a	6 - f	11 - k	16 - p	21 - u	24 - x
2 - b	7 - g	12 - l	17 - q	22 - v	25 - y
3 - c	8 - h	13 - m	18 - r	23 - w	26 - z
4 - d	9 - i	14 - n	19 - s		
5 - e	10 - j	15 - o	20 - t		

Write the letters under the numbers below to crack the code.

20 - 8 - 5 - 3 - 12 - 1 - 19 - 19 - 23 - 9 - 12 - 12 - 12 - 9 - 14 - 5 - 21 - 16 - 23 - 8 - 5 - 14 - 20 -

8 - 5 - 6 - 9 - 18 - 5 - 4 - 18 - 9 - 12 - 12 - 2 - 5 - 7 - 9 - 14 - 19.

16 - 21 - 20 - 20 - 8 - 5 - 16 - 1 - 16 - 5 - 18 - 1 - 14 - 4 - 16 - 5 - 14 - 3 - 9 - 12 - 15 - 14 - 20 -

8 - 5 - 4 - 5 - 19 - 11.

20 - 8 - 5 - 20 - 5 - 1 - 3 - 8 - 5 - 18 - 23 - 18 - 9 - 20 - 5 - 19 - 15 - 14 - 20 - 8 - 5 - 2 - 15 - 1 -

18 - 4 - 23 - 9 - 20 - 8 - 3 - 8 - 1 - 12 - 11.

20 - 8 - 5 - 1 - 21 - 4 - 9 - 20 - 15 - 18 - 9 - 21 - 13 - 9 - 19 - 14 - 5 - 24 - 20 - 20 - 15 - 20 -

8 - 5 - 7 - 25 - 13.

23 - 5 - 5 - 1 - 20 - 9 - 14 - 20 - 8 - 5 - 3 - 1 - 6 - 5 - 20 - 5 - 18 - 9 - 1.

20 - 8 - 5 - 16 - 18 - 9 - 14 - 3 - 9 - 16 - 1 - 12 - 1 - 14 - 4 - 20 - 8 - 5 - 14 - 21 - 18 - 19 - 5 -

1 - 18 - 5 - 9 - 14 - 20 - 8 - 5 - 15 - 6 - 6 - 9 - 3 - 5.

On the back of this page, write your own coded message. Ask your partner to crack it.

Survival Vocabulary

Sentence Sense

Read each sentence. One of the three sentences sounds correct. Circle the letter in front of the correct sentence.

1. (a) Our school has many class for the students to sit at.
   (b) Our class always eats lunch together at noon.
   (c) Let's all go to the gym to play class today.

2. (a) My teacher always takes time to explain the directions.
   (b) Please take me to the teacher to get a bandage for my arm.
   (c) The teacher is the head person in the whole school.

3. (a) Please take these students to the period down this hall.
   (b) I'm not sure which period I have science.
   (c) Please write on the period so the whole class may see.

4. (a) I write my homework in my auditorium.
   (b) Our class likes to hear the auditorium speak.
   (c) Please show that boy where the auditorium is.

5. (a) I like to sit with my cafeteria in class.
   (b) The cafeteria always rings before school starts in the morning.
   (c) I'll take you to the cafeteria for lunch.

6. (a) You may write on this nice, clean fire drill.
   (b) We must leave the school building when there is a fire drill.
   (c) I saw the fire drill burning a few minutes ago.

7. (a) Our teacher told us to use the computer for that work.
   (b) I'm glad our computer didn't give us a test today.
   (c) The students should make a computer while waiting for lunch.

8. (a) Make sure you're sitting at your desk when the bell rings.
   (b) I like to write with colored desk at the board.
   (c) Here comes the desk to talk to our class.

9. (a) My teacher always uses pencil to write with at the board.
   (b) Every student should bring a pencil to school.
   (c) Please write all those spelling words in a list on that pencil.

(continued)

Sentence Sense *(continued)*

10. (a) I've written so many sentences on this paper.
    (b) You may do your schoolwork at home as paper.
    (c) The paper will ring in a few minutes.

11. (a) We may use the office today to take our gym class.
    (b) The principal will office the students every day.
    (c) I like to take the banking and lunch money to the office.

12. (a) The principal is the only person who helps us when we're sick.
    (b) The principal always fixes the students' lunches.
    (c) The principal in our school is the boss of the building.

13. (a) We find lots of information on the Internet.
    (b) Be sure to get in line when you hear the Internet.
    (c) I finished all of my Internet at school today.

14. (a) Please bring this letter to the lady in the bell.
    (b) The bell will ring at nine o'clock.
    (c) There are twenty-five students in our bell.

15. (a) I like to have math class during third software.
    (b) The software is the head person in the school.
    (c) We have software in our school for creating newsletters.

16. (a) We always do lots of exercises in the gym.
    (b) The gym is a quiet place to rest when you are sick.
    (c) Be sure to finish all of your gym before coming to school.

17. (a) The microchip entered our class at two o'clock.
    (b) The principal spoke into the microchip during the assembly.
    (c) Each microchip provides the computer with a link between two points.

18. (a) We must get to school before the board rings.
    (b) Our teacher lets us write our words on the board.
    (c) She has reading during fourth board.

19. (a) Please show her how to sit up straight at the chalk.
    (b) She asked us to write all our sentences on the chalk.
    (c) Please hand me that piece of chalk to use at the board.

20. (a) I like to do my homework as soon as I'm finished with supper.
    (b) Please take this note to the homework for the teacher.
    (c) Let's get in homework and wait for the bell to ring.

Pen the Pig

1. Divide the list of words in Exercise 1 into two lists of ten words each.
2. Choose a partner. Give your partner one of the lists of ten words. You keep the other list.
3. Say one of the words on your list. Your partner writes it down on a sheet of paper.
4. You check your partner's spelling.
5. If the word is spelled correctly, your partner may touch his or her pencil to a dot and draw one straight line across or down to another dot.
6. If the word is not spelled correctly, your partner may not draw a line.
7. Now your partner says one of the words on his or her list to you. You write it down.
8. Your partner checks the spelling.
9. If the word is spelled correctly, you may draw one line between two dots, going across or down.
10. If the word is not spelled correctly, you may not draw a line.
11. You and your partner take turns saying and writing words. Say a new word on the list each time.
12. Each time you draw a line, you are building a pen for the pig.
13. The object of this game is to be the person to draw the **last** line to make a square. This square is one pen. Put your initials in that pen. That pen is yours.
14. Watch the lines. Try to be the **last** person to draw the line to make a square.
15. When you and your partner have each written ten words, switch lists. Take turns saying and writing words again. Decide how many times you want to switch lists.
16. When you have finished switching lists, or when there are no more dots to use, the game is over.
17. Count the number of squares holding your initials.
18. The person with the most pens wins.

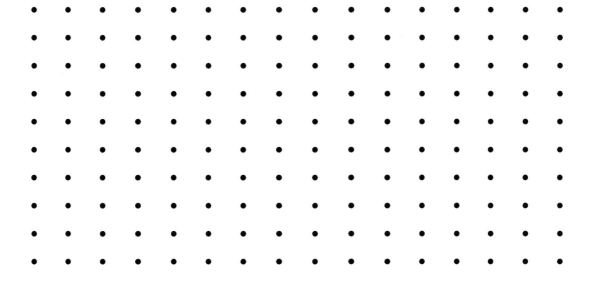

Backward Puzzle

Write a brief definition or clue for each word in the puzzle.

1.				g	y	m				1. _____
2.				o	f	f	i	c	e	2. _____
3.	c	o	m	p	u	t	e	r		3. _____
4.	p	e	n	c	i	l				4. _____
5.		f	i	r	e	d	r	i	l	l	5. _____
6.		t	e	a	c	h	e	r		6. _____
7.	i	n	t	e	r	n	e	t		7. _____
8.	p	r	i	n	c	i	p	a	l	8. _____
9.		b	o	a	r	d				9. _____
10.		b	e	l	l					10. _____
11.	h	o	m	e	w	o	r	k		11. _____
12.		s	o	f	t	w	a	r	e	12. _____
13.		p	a	p	e	r				13. _____
14.	c	a	f	e	t	e	r	i	a	14. _____
15.		d	e	s	k					15. _____
16.	m	i	c	r	o	c	h	i	p	16. _____
17.		c	h	a	l	k				17. _____
18.	p	e	r	i	o	d				18. _____
19.	a	u	d	i	t	o	r	i	u	m	19. _____
20.		c	l	a	s	s				20. _____

Find the hidden sentence that reads from the top down in the puzzle.
Write it here.

_____

Sneaky Snakes

Dissect (cut apart) these snakes by drawing lines through their bodies after every word. Write your starting, finishing, and total times for each snake. Try to do each snake faster than the last one.

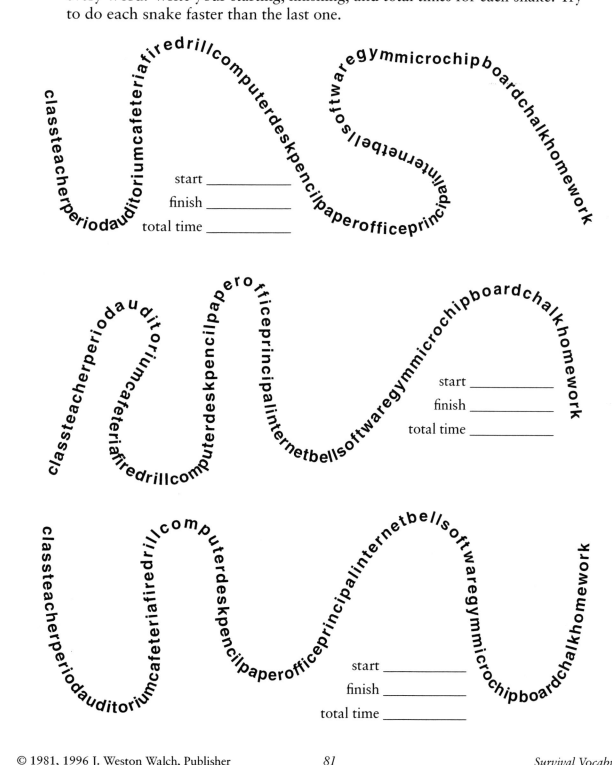

start _____

finish _____

total time _____

start _____

finish _____

total time _____

start _____

finish _____

total time _____

X-ray Vision

Write each word correctly.   **Write the words in alphabetical order.**

1. claass   _____   _____

2. teechur   _____   _____

3. peereud   _____   _____

4. awditohreeum   _____   _____

5. kaffiteereeuh   _____   _____

6. fiur duryl   _____   _____

7. campewtor   _____   _____

8. dezzk   _____   _____

9. pensul   _____   _____

10. paapur   _____   _____

11. awfiss   _____   _____

12. prinsipul   _____   _____

13. innturnyt   _____   _____

14. belll   _____   _____

15. sawfwhere   _____   _____

16. jim   _____   _____

17. mycrowgip   _____   _____

18. bord   _____   _____

19. chauk   _____   _____

20. homwurk   _____   _____

               Survival Vocabulary

Silly Dilly

Write a story using all of the following words. Make it interesting!

1. class	6. fire drill	11. office	16. gym
2. teacher	7. computer	12. principal	17. microchip
3. period	8. desk	13. Internet	18. board
4. auditorium	9. pencil	14. bell	19. chalk
5. cafeteria	10. paper	15. software	20. homework

_____

_____

_____

_____

_____

_____

_____

_____

_____

_____

_____

_____

_____

_____

_____

_____

Unit 7
Health Words

ambulance	doctor	hospital
lab technician	nurse	bandage
appointment	sick	healthy
midwife	hurt	antiseptic
sore	clinic	ache
vitamin	dentist	sprain
medicine		emergency

New Words and Lost Letters

Read each word and its definition. In the Lost Letters column, write each word by filling in the missing letters.

LOST LETTERS

1.	healthy	being well; a good condition of the body	heal _ _ y
2.	doctor	a person trained to treat people who are sick or hurt	doc _ _ _
3.	sick	having some illness or disease	_ _ ck
4.	ache	a dull pain that lasts for a while	a _ h _
5.	hurt	to have pain	hu _ _
6.	sore	painful	so _ _
7.	sprain	an injury caused by sudden twisting	_ _ rain
8.	clinic	a place where sick people are treated and released	_ _ _ nic
9.	hospital	a place where sick people are cared for and may stay overnight	_ _ _ p _ t _ _
10.	ambulance	a van for bringing sick or injured people to the hospital	_ mb _ _ _ nce
11.	emergency	something serious that happens suddenly and calls for fast action	_ m _ r _ _ nc _
12.	vitamin	a substance needed for normal body growth and health	v _ t _ m _ n
13.	antiseptic	something that kills germs	ant _ _ ep _ _ c
14.	bandage	a cover for a cut or other injury	ba _ _ ag _
15.	appointment	an arrangement to be somewhere at a certain time	a _ _ oi _ _ m _ n _
16.	nurse	a person who takes care of the sick	n _ _ _ _
17.	lab technician	a person who tests blood and other samples	l _ b t _ _ h _ ic _ _ n
18.	midwife	a person who helps women give birth	mi _ _ _ f _
19.	dentist	a doctor whose work is caring for teeth	d _ _ _ ist
20.	medicine	something to help improve or cure an illness or disease	med _ c _ _ _

Survival Vocabulary

Snoop and Solve

Find the words in the maze and circle them. The words may go across, up, down, or diagonally. Check them off in the list at the top as you find them.

___ 1. healthy	___ 8. clinic	___ 15. appointment
___ 2. doctor	___ 9. hospital	___ 16. nurse
___ 3. sick	___ 10. ambulance	___ 17. lab technician
___ 4. ache	___ 11. emergency	___ 18. midwife
___ 5. hurt	___ 12. vitamin	___ 19. dentist
___ 6. sore	___ 13. antiseptic	___ 20. medicine
___ 7. sprain	___ 14. bandage	

a	l	l	a	b	k	m	e	d	i	c	i	n	e
c	a	a	h	e	a	l	t	h	y	s	o	r	s
h	t	b	g	u	c	n	c	m	c	l	o	d	o
i	i	t	a	o	r	i	d	c	l	s	a	i	y
e	p	e	r	p	n	t	e	a	s	p	c	s	c
c	s	c	g	i	p	d	n	e	g	t	h	m	n
n	o	h	l	b	a	o	t	n	r	e	e	i	e
a	h	n	e	n	k	c	i	p	a	r	m	d	g
l	c	i	t	c	c	t	s	n	p	a	n	w	r
u	l	c	i	e	a	o	t	e	t	i	r	i	e
b	i	i	e	e	p	r	c	i	a	m	v	f	m
m	n	a	h	a	e	i	v	r	e	o	e	e	e
a	i	n	u	r	s	e	p	s	i	c	k	n	l
d	c	a	n	t	i	s	e	p	t	i	c	o	t

Scrambled Eggs

Write the words correctly.   **Divide the words into syllables.**

1. thyealh   _____   _____

2. oorctd   _____   _____

3. cksi   _____   _____

4. chea   _____   _____

5. urht   _____   _____

6. reso   _____   _____

7. airnps   _____   _____

8. iicnlc   _____   _____

9. pilatosh   _____   _____

10. lambanuce   _____   _____

11. greenycem   _____   _____

12. amintiv   _____   _____

13. panicesitt   _____   _____

14. aaegdnb   _____   _____

15. ppointenmta   _____   _____

16. surne   _____   _____

17. alb chictenian   _____   _____

18. fewmidi   _____   _____

19. ttiends   _____   _____

20. mideince   _____   _____

 Survival Vocabulary

Pick a Pair

Write the number of each definition in front of the word it goes with.

_____ healthy

_____ doctor

_____ sick

_____ ache

_____ hurt

_____ sore

_____ sprain

_____ clinic

_____ hospital

_____ ambulance

_____ emergency

_____ vitamin

_____ antiseptic

_____ bandage

_____ appointment

_____ nurse

_____ lab technician

_____ midwife

_____ dentist

_____ medicine

1. to have pain

2. a person trained to treat people who are sick or hurt

3. something to help improve or cure an illness or disease

4. a place where sick people are cared for and may stay overnight

5. a cover for a cut or other injury

6. painful

7. a person who helps women give birth

8. having some illness or disease

9. being well; a good condition of the body

10. an injury caused by sudden twisting

11. a van for bringing sick or injured people to the hospital

12. a dull pain that lasts for a while

13. a doctor whose work is caring for teeth

14. a person who takes care of the sick

15. something that kills germs

16. something serious that happens suddenly and calls for fast action

17. a place where sick people are treated and released

18. a substance needed for normal body growth and health

19. an arrangement to be somewhere at a certain time

20. a person who tests blood and other samples

Crack the Code

1 - a	6 - f	11 - k	16 - p	21 - u	24 - x
2 - b	7 - g	12 - l	17 - q	22 - v	25 - y
3 - c	8 - h	13 - m	18 - r	23 - w	26 - z
4 - d	9 - i	14 - n	19 - s		
5 - e	10 - j	15 - o	20 - t		

Write the letters under the numbers below to crack the code.

5 - 1 - 20 - 7 - 15 - 15 - 4 - 6 - 15 - 15 - 4 - 20 - 15 - 2 - 5 - 8 - 5 - 1 - 12 - 20 - 8 - 25.

19 - 9 - 3 - 11 - 16 - 5 - 15 - 16 - 12 - 5 - 19 - 5 - 5 - 1 - 4 - 15 - 3 - 20 - 15 - 18 - 6 - 15 - 18 -

8 - 5 - 12 - 16.

3 - 15 - 22 - 5 - 18 - 1 - 3 - 21 - 20 - 23 - 9 - 20 - 8 - 1 - 2 - 1 - 14 - 4 - 1 - 7 - 5.

20 - 1 - 11 - 5 - 20 - 8 - 5 - 13 - 5 - 4 - 9 - 3 - 9 - 14 - 5 - 1 - 19 - 20 - 8 - 5 - 4 - 5 - 14 - 20 - 9 -

19 - 20 - 19 - 1 - 9 - 4.

13 - 1 - 11 - 5 - 20 - 8 - 5 - 1 - 16 - 16 - 15 - 9 - 14 - 20 - 13 - 5 - 14 - 20 - 6 - 15 - 18 - 20 -

23 - 15 - 15 - 3 - 12 - 15 - 3 - 11.

7 - 15 - 20 - 15 - 20 - 8 - 5 - 3 - 12 - 9 - 14 - 9 - 3 - 9 - 6 - 25 - 15 - 21 - 18 - 20 - 8 - 18 - 15 -

1 - 20 - 9 - 19 - 19 - 20 - 9 - 12 - 12 - 19 - 15 - 18 - 5.

On the back of this page, write your own coded message. Ask your partner to crack it.

 Survival Vocabulary

Sentence Sense

Read each sentence. One of the three sentences sounds correct. Circle the letter in front of the correct sentence.

1. (a) His body is strong and healthy because he eats well.
   (b) Please take me to the healthy to buy some medicine.
   (c) I take some healthy when my throat hurts.

2. (a) Please help me put this doctor on my sore arm to protect it.
   (b) The person standing at the table is the doctor.
   (c) I'll fill the doctor with ice while you hold the pack.

3. (a) My mother is a very sick person.
   (b) The sick on my foot hurts all the time.
   (c) We can take him to the sick to get help for his cut.

4. (a) Please give her this gargle to ache with every morning.
   (b) Many medicines are sold at the ache on the corner.
   (c) The ache in my arm hurt me all night and all day.

5. (a) My father told me his stomach hurt after he ate that food.
   (b) Please put this hurt over the bruise on my knee.
   (c) My hurt with the doctor is for tomorrow morning.

6. (a) My brother said that his shoulder is sore.
   (b) Take one teaspoon of sore each time you eat a meal.
   (c) The sore will see us at noon tomorrow.

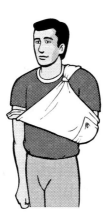

7. (a) I take a sprain with my food to help keep me healthy.
   (b) The sprain on this street is the one my family goes to.
   (c) The sprain in my wrist hurts when I try to write.

8. (a) We took that family of eight people to the clinic for a checkup.
   (b) That clinic on my foot needs to be changed.
   (c) I feel so clinic when I get tired.

9. (a) Let's arrange a hospital to see the doctor next week.
   (b) We should be quiet when visiting in a hospital.
   (c) He brought a bottle of hospital to help me get better.

(continued)

Sentence Sense *(continued)*

10. (a) Many people have been taken to the hospital by that ambulance.
    (b) I eat good food to stay good and ambulance.
    (c) That large ambulance on my knee still hurts when I walk.

11. (a) Please come to the emergency room with me.
    (b) I plugged in the emergency so it would get warm.
    (c) Don't take too much emergency or you'll be sick.

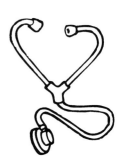

12. (a) She takes a vitamin with every meal she eats.
    (b) Please help him vitamin her sore arm.
    (c) I felt so vitamin last night because I ate too much.

13. (a) Please ask him to bandage my head with that antiseptic.
    (b) Please hand me that antiseptic on the table.
    (c) We can take them to the antiseptic to get help for his sister.

14. (a) Please show her how to gargle with the bandage now.
    (b) I'll help you change the bandage on the little boy's foot.
    (c) The dentist gave him some medicine to bandage.

15. (a) I made an appointment with the doctor for next Monday.
    (b) The appointment on my hand hurts when I move my fingers.
    (c) The appointment shows us how to take care of our teeth.

16. (a) We are visiting our aunt at the lab technician today.
    (b) She brought a lab technician for me to use on my sprained ankle.
    (c) A lab technician will take samples for testing.

17. (a) The midwife is the person to see for my sore back.
    (b) They went to the midwife when the baby was due.
    (c) Let's go to the midwife to see the dentist.

18. (a) Please help me nurse the clinic for all those people.
    (b) My throat feels so much better after I nurse with this medicine.
    (c) The nurse will be back at two o'clock on Friday.

19. (a) My dentist cleaned my teeth on Friday.
    (b) That dentist will heat up quickly after it's plugged in.
    (c) Good food helps my body stay nice and dentist.

20. (a) The medicine is the large white building on the corner.
    (b) Make sure you take your medicine as the doctor said.
    (c) The medicine closes at ten o'clock every day.

Pen the Pig

1. Divide the list of words in Exercise 1 into two lists of ten words each.
2. Choose a partner. Give your partner one of the lists of ten words. You keep the other list.
3. Say one of the words on your list. Your partner writes it down on a sheet of paper.
4. You check your partner's spelling.
5. If the word is spelled correctly, your partner may touch his or her pencil to a dot and draw one straight line across or down to another dot.
6. If the word is not spelled correctly, your partner may not draw a line.
7. Now your partner says one of the words on his or her list to you. You write it down.
8. Your partner checks the spelling.
9. If the word is spelled correctly, you may draw one line between two dots, going across or down.
10. If the word is not spelled correctly, you may not draw a line.
11. You and your partner take turns saying and writing words. Say a new word on the list each time.
12. Each time you draw a line, you are building a pen for the pig.
13. The object of this game is to be the person to draw the **last** line to make a square. This square is one pen. Put your initials in that pen. That pen is yours.
14. Watch the lines. Try to be the **last** person to draw the line to make a square.
15. When you and your partner have each written ten words, switch lists. Take turns saying and writing words again. Decide how many times you want to switch lists.
16. When you have finished switching lists, or when there are no more dots to use, the game is over.
17. Count the number of squares holding your initials.
18. The person with the most pens wins.

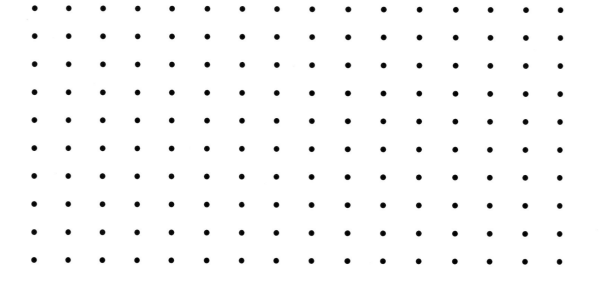

Backward Puzzle

Write a brief definition or clue for each word in the puzzle.

#	Word	#	Clue
1.	a n t i s e p t i c	1.	_____
2.	h o s p i t a l	2.	_____
3.	d o c t o r	3.	_____
4.	s i c k	4.	_____
5.	h u r t	5.	_____
6.	n u r s e	6.	_____
7.	a m b u l a n c e	7.	_____
8.	h e a l t h y	8.	_____
9.	d e n t i s t	9.	_____
10.	l a b t e c h n i c i a n	10.	_____
11.	s o r e	11.	_____
12.	v i t a m i n	12.	_____
13.	e m e r g e n c y	13.	_____
14.	s p r a i n	14.	_____
15.	m i d w i f e	15.	_____
16.	m e d i c i n e	16.	_____
17.	b a n d a g e	17.	_____
18.	c l i n i c	18.	_____
19.	a p p o i n t m e n t	19.	_____
20.	a c h e	20.	_____

Find the hidden sentence that reads from the top down in the puzzle.
Write it here.

_____

94   *Survival Vocabulary*

Sneaky Snakes

Dissect (cut apart) these snakes by drawing lines through their bodies after every word. Write your starting, finishing, and total times for each snake. Try to do each snake faster than the last one.

healthydoctorsickachehurtsoresprainclinichospitalambulanceemergencyvitaminantisepticbandageappointmentnurselabtechnicianmidwifedentistmedicine

start _____

finish _____

total time _____

start _____

finish _____

total time _____

healthydoctorsickachehurtsoresprainclinichospitalambulanceemergencyvitaminantisepticbandageappointmentnurselabtechnicianmidwifedentistmedicine

healthydoctorsickachehurtsoresprainclinichospitalambulanceemergencyvitaminantisepticbandageappointmentnurselabtechnicianmidwifedentistmedicine

start _____

finish _____

total time _____

X-ray Vision

Write each word correctly.   **Write the words in alphabetical order.**

1. helthee   _____   _____

2. dokter   _____   _____

3. sik   _____   _____

4. aik   _____   _____

5. hert   _____   _____

6. soar   _____   _____

7. sprayn   _____   _____

8. klinik   _____   _____

9. hospittle   _____   _____

10. ambyulaanse   _____   _____

11. eemurjensee   _____   _____

12. vitamen   _____   _____

13. antissepptik   _____   _____

14. bandedge   _____   _____

15. apoyntmunt   _____   _____

16. nerse   _____   _____

17. labe teknision   _____   _____

18. medwyfe   _____   _____

19. denntissed   _____   _____

20. medesin   _____   _____

Silly Dilly

Write a story using all of the following words. Make it interesting!

1. healthy	6. sore	11. emergency	16. nurse
2. doctor	7. sprain	12. vitamin	17. lab technician
3. sick	8. clinic	13. antiseptic	18. midwife
4. ache	9. hospital	14. bandage	19. dentist
5. hurt	10. ambulance	15. appointment	20. medicine

_____

_____

_____

_____

_____

_____

_____

_____

_____

_____

_____

_____

_____

_____

_____

Unit 8
Community Words

post office	barber	sidewalk
police officer	synagogue	mailbox
theater	church	pharmacy
superintendent	laundry	plumber
fire station	school	garage
factory	mall	library
restaurant		bank

New Words and Lost Letters

Read each word and its definition. In the Lost Letters column, write each word by filling in the missing letters.

LOST LETTERS

1.	factory	a place where things are made	fa _ _ _ r _
2.	garage	a building where cars are parked or repaired	_ ar _ _ _
3.	laundry	a place where clothes and linens are washed	l _ _ n _ r _
4.	pharmacy	a store where medicine is sold	p _ a _ mac _
5.	sidewalk	a place at the side of a street where people can walk	_ id _ _ a _ _
6.	synagogue	a building where Jews worship	s _ _ _ gog _ _
7.	church	a building where Christians worship	_ _ urch
8.	police officer	a person who keeps order	_ _ li _ _ _ ff _ _ er
9.	fire station	a building for people and equipment that put out fires	_ _ re _ ta _ _ on
10.	post office	a place where mail is handled and postage stamps are sold	_ _ st off _ _ _
11.	mall	a large building containing a variety of shops	m _ _ l
12.	mailbox	a box from which mail is collected or to which mail is delivered	_ _ _ lb _ x
13.	barber	a person who cuts other people's hair	_ _ _ ber
14.	superintendent	a person who oversees something or is in charge of an apartment building	s _ p _ r _ nt _ _ d _ _ t
15.	plumber	a person who installs and repairs pipes	pl _ _ _ er
16.	restaurant	a place to buy and eat a meal	_ _ st _ _ ran _
17.	theater	a place were movies are shown	t _ _ ate _
18.	bank	a place for saving, borrowing, or exchanging money	_ _ nk
19.	school	a place for teaching and learning	_ _ hoo _
20.	library	a place where many books are kept	_ _ _ rar _

Snoop and Solve

Find the words in the maze and circle them. The words may go across, up, down, or diagonally. Check them off in the list at the top as you find them.

___ 1. factory   ___ 8. police officer   ___ 15. plumber

___ 2. garage   ___ 9. fire station   ___ 16. restaurant

___ 3. laundry   ___ 10. post office   ___ 17. theater

___ 4. pharmacy   ___ 11. mall   ___ 18. bank

___ 5. sidewalk   ___ 12. mailbox   ___ 19. school

___ 6. synagogue   ___ 13. barber   ___ 20. library

___ 7. church   ___ 14. superintendent

r	a	b	n	o	f	s	c	h	o	o	l	p	r
p	p	h	a	r	m	a	c	y	z	a	i	o	e
b	a	l	b	e	f	e	c	d	b	k	b	s	c
q	t	l	c	u	i	u	l	t	n	b	r	t	i
r	n	a	k	g	r	d	g	a	o	a	a	o	f
l	a	m	d	o	e	g	b	s	x	r	r	f	f
r	r	a	l	g	s	a	a	i	t	b	y	f	o
e	u	i	a	a	t	r	r	d	c	e	i	i	e
b	a	l	u	n	a	a	e	e	h	r	r	c	c
m	t	b	n	y	t	g	t	w	u	m	n	e	i
u	s	o	d	s	i	e	a	a	r	r	c	o	l
l	e	x	r	x	o	o	e	l	c	e	z	p	o
p	r	u	y	g	n	i	h	k	h	p	x	c	p
s	u	p	e	r	i	n	t	e	n	d	e	n	t

Name _____

Date _____

Scrambled Eggs

Write the words correctly.   **Divide the words into syllables.**

1. fortyac   _____   _____

2. aggare   _____   _____

3. drulyan   _____   _____

4. camphary   _____   _____

5. kladesiw   _____   _____

6. ynsgogaue   _____   _____

7. chruhc   _____   _____

8. ecilpo rofeifc _____   _____

9. ifre notaits   _____   _____

10. pots ffoice   _____   _____

11. amla   _____   _____

12. boxmlia   _____   _____

13. rrbbae   _____   _____

14. tenprideenntsu _____   _____

15. bluprem   _____   _____

16. ranttauser   _____   _____

17. eaterth   _____   _____

18. anbk   _____   _____

19. loohsc   _____   _____

20. yrrailb   _____   _____

               Survival Vocabulary

Pick a Pair

Write the number of each definition in front of the word it goes with.

____ factory

____ garage

____ laundry

____ pharmacy

____ sidewalk

____ synagogue

____ church

____ police officer

____ fire station

____ post office

____ mall

____ mailbox

____ barber

____ superintendent

____ plumber

____ restaurant

____ theater

____ bank

____ school

____ library

1. a place at the side of a street where people can walk

2. a place where mail is handled and postage stamps are sold

3. a person who installs and repairs pipes

4. a store where medicine is sold

5. a place where many books are kept

6. a place where movies are shown

7. a place where things are made

8. a building where Christians worship

9. a person who oversees something or is in charge of an apartment building

10. a large building containing a variety of shops

11. a person who keeps order

12. a place for teaching and learning

13. a place for saving, borrowing, or exchanging money

14. a building where cars are parked or repaired

15. a place where clothes and linens are washed

16. a building where Jews worship

17. a building for people and equipment that put out fires

18. a place to buy and eat a meal

19. a person who cuts other people's hair

20. a box from which mail is collected or to which mail is delivered

Crack the Code

1 - a	6 - f	11 - k	16 - p	21 - u	24 - x
2 - b	7 - g	12 - l	17 - q	22 - v	25 - y
3 - c	8 - h	13 - m	18 - r	23 - w	26 - z
4 - d	9 - i	14 - n	19 - s		
5 - e	10 - j	15 - o	20 - t		

Write the letters under the numbers below to crack the code.

23 - 5 - 20 - 1 - 11 - 5 - 15 - 21 - 18 - 19 - 8 - 5 - 5 - 20 - 19 - 20 - 15 - 20 - 8 - 1 - 20 - 12 -

1 - 21 - 14 - 4 - 18 - 25.

20 - 8 - 1 - 20 - 20 - 8 - 5 - 1 - 20 - 5 - 18 - 9 - 19 - 19 - 8 - 15 - 23 - 9 - 14 - 7 - 1 - 6 - 21 - 14 -

14 - 25 - 6 - 9 - 12 - 13.

15 - 21 - 18 - 12 - 9 - 2 - 18 - 1 - 18 - 25 - 8 - 1 - 19 - 19 - 15 - 13 - 1 - 14 - 25 - 2 - 15 - 15-

11 - 19.

20 - 8 - 1 - 20 - 16 - 15 - 12 - 9 - 3 - 5 - 15 - 6 - 6 - 9 - 3 - 5 - 18 - 19 - 20 - 15 - 16 - 16 - 5 -

4 - 20 - 8 - 5 - 6 - 9 - 7 - 8 - 20.

20 - 8 - 5 - 18 - 5 - 9 - 19 - 1 - 12 - 1 - 18 - 7 - 5 - 7 - 1 - 18 - 1 - 7 - 5 - 14 - 5 - 24 - 20 - 20 -

15 - 20 - 8 - 5 - 6 - 1 - 3 - 20 - 15 - 18 - 25.

23 - 5 - 18 - 9 - 4 - 5 - 1 - 2 - 21 - 19 - 20 - 15 - 7 - 5 - 20 - 20 - 15 - 19 - 3 - 8 - 15 - 15 - 12.

On the back of this page, write your own coded message. Ask your partner to crack it.

               Survival Vocabulary

Sentence Sense

Read each sentence. One of the three sentences sounds correct. Circle the letter in front of the correct sentence.

1. (a) I'm going to the factory to borrow some money.
   (b) My sister works in the factory on the corner.
   (c) That factory will help us put out the fire.

2. (a) She will have her car fixed at the garage.
   (b) She will garage the children.
   (c) My dad borrowed a garage at the library.

3. (a) I'm getting my hair cut at the laundry.
   (b) We can buy many different foods at the laundry.
   (c) We take our clothes to the laundry to be washed.

4. (a) There's a good movie playing at the pharmacy.
   (b) She needs to mail that pharmacy today.
   (c) I'm going to the pharmacy to buy some medicine.

5. (a) We can walk on the sidewalk to stay out of the mud.
   (b) That sidewalk sells shirts and shoes.
   (c) We can ride the sidewalk to school.

6. (a) My father mailed the letters at the synagogue.
   (b) Christians worship in a synagogue.
   (c) The synagogue is large enough for those Jewish people.

7. (a) Many Christians worship in that church.
   (b) He's having his hair cut in the church.
   (c) Jewish people worship in that church.

8. (a) The bakery sells that police officer.
   (b) The police officer helped the man in the car accident.
   (c) The police officer is where we can borrow books.

9. (a) The movies are shown at the fire station.
   (b) Baked foods are sold at the fire station.
   (c) The fire station helped put out that fire quickly.

(continued)

         Survival Vocabulary

Sentence Sense *(continued)*

10. (a) We'll buy stamps for the letters at the post office.
    (b) He went to the post office to buy medicine.
    (c) The post office sells baked foods.

11. (a) We can eat the mall for breakfast.
    (b) The letter carrier brought the mall to our house.
    (c) The mall is a good place to shop.

12. (a) We went to the mailbox to buy bread.
    (b) Please put all the food in the mailbox.
    (c) That mailbox is full of mail.

13. (a) The barber cut my brother's hair.
    (b) We went to the barber to borrow some books.
    (c) The barber's job is to put out fires.

14. (a) The superintendent is a place to worship.
    (b) We can buy and eat a meal at the superintendent.
    (c) Our superintendent takes care of our apartment building.

15. (a) The plumber carries mail to our home.
    (b) Our broken pipes were fixed by the plumber.
    (c) Please park your car in that plumber down the street.

16. (a) I love to eat at that restaurant.
    (b) That restaurant was mailed to my friend.
    (c) The barber cut the restaurant's hair.

17. (a) That theater shows good movies.
    (b) Please mail those letters at the theater.
    (c) People buy medicine at the theater.

18. (a) Some people have their hair cut at that bank.
    (b) We keep our money in that bank.
    (c) Let's have supper in the bank on the corner.

19. (a) That girl buys food for her family at the school.
    (b) You may mail the school at the post office.
    (c) The students learn many things at school.

20. (a) It's fun to borrow books at the library.
    (b) She bought some bread for her family at the library.
    (c) My mother is in the library because she's sick.

Pen the Pig

1. Divide the list of words in Exercise 1 into two lists of ten words each.
2. Choose a partner. Give your partner one of the lists of ten words. You keep the other list.
3. Say one of the words on your list. Your partner writes it down on a sheet of paper.
4. You check your partner's spelling.
5. If the word is spelled correctly, your partner may touch his or her pencil to a dot and draw one straight line across or down to another dot.
6. If the word is not spelled correctly, your partner may not draw a line.
7. Now your partner says one of the words on his or her list to you. You write it down.
8. Your partner checks the spelling.
9. If the word is spelled correctly, you may draw one line between two dots, going across or down.
10. If the word is not spelled correctly, you may not draw a line.
11. You and your partner take turns saying and writing words. Say a new word on the list each time.
12. Each time you draw a line, you are building a pen for the pig.
13. The object of this game is to be the person to draw the **last** line to make a square. This square is one pen. Put your initials in that pen. That pen is yours.
14. Watch the lines. Try to be the **last** person to draw the line to make a square.
15. When you and your partner have each written ten words, switch lists. Take turns saying and writing words again. Decide how many times you want to switch lists.
16. When you have finished switching lists, or when there are no more dots to use, the game is over.
17. Count the number of squares holding your initials.
18. The person with the most pens wins.

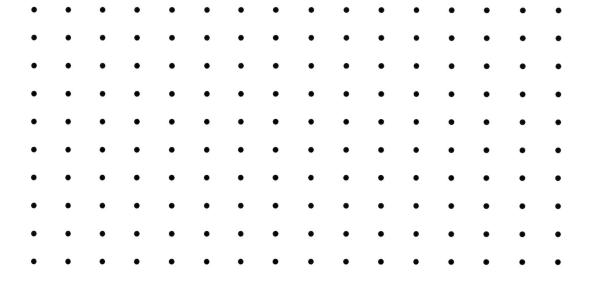

Backward Puzzle

Write a brief definition or clue for each word in the puzzle.

1.			g	a	r	a	g	e					1.	_____
2.			b	a	r	b	e	r					2.	_____
3.		f	i	r	e	s	t	a	t	i	o	n	3.	_____
4.			t	h	e	a	t	e	r				4.	_____
5.			s	c	h	o	o	l					5.	_____
6.			b	a	n	k							6.	_____
7.			l	a	u	n	d	r	y				7.	_____
8.	p	o	l	i	c	e	o	f	f	i	c	e	r	8.	_____
9.			s	i	d	e	w	a	l	k			9.	_____
10.			r	e	s	t	a	u	r	a	n	t	10.	_____
11.				c	h	u	r	c	h				11.	_____
					e									
12.				f	a	c	t	o	r	y			12.	_____
13.		s	y	n	a	g	o	g	u	e			13.	_____
14.					m	a	l	l					14.	_____
15.			p	h	a	r	m	a	c	y			15.	_____
16.				p	l	u	m	b	e	r			16.	_____
17.	s	u	p	e	r	i	n	t	e	n	d	e	n	t	17.	_____
18.				m	a	i	l	b	o	x			18.	_____
19.			p	o	s	t	o	f	f	i	c	e	19.	_____
20.	l	i	b	r	a	r	y						20.	_____

Find the hidden sentence that reads from the top down in the puzzle.
Write it here.

_____

Sneaky Snakes

Dissect (cut apart) these snakes by drawing lines through their bodies after every word. Write your starting, finishing, and total times for each snake. Try to do each snake faster than the last one.

factorygaragelaundrypharmacysidewalksynagoguechurchpoliceofficerfirestationpostofficemailboxbarbersuperintendentplumberrestauranttheaterbankschoollibrary

start _____

finish _____

total time _____

factorygaragelaundrypharmacysidewalksynagoguechurchpoliceofficerfirestationpostofficemallmailboxbarbersuperintendentplumberrestauranttheaterbankschoollibrary

start _____

finish _____

total time _____

factorygaragelaundrypharmacysidewalksynagoguechurchpoliceofficerfirestationpostofficemallmailboxbarbersuperintendentplumberrestauranttheaterbankschoollibrary

start _____

finish _____

total time _____

X-ray Vision

Write each word correctly.   **Write the words in alphabetical order.**

1. faktohree   _____   _____

2. gahrahj   _____   _____

3. lawndree   _____   _____

4. pharmercy   _____   _____

5. siidwauk   _____   _____

6. sinagahg   _____   _____

7. chirrch   _____   _____

8. pahlees awfisir   _____   _____

9. fiir stayshun   _____   _____

10. posst awfiss   _____   _____

11. mawel   _____   _____

12. maylbahx   _____   _____

13. barrburr   _____   _____

14. soupirintendunt   _____   _____

15. pluhmir   _____   _____

16. resstrahnt   _____   _____

17. theeahtur   _____   _____

18. baynk   _____   _____

19. skool   _____   _____

20. librahree   _____   _____

Silly Dilly

Write a story using all of the following words. Make it interesting!

1. factory	6. synagogue	11. mall	16. restaurant
2. garage	7. church	12. mailbox	17. theater
3. laundry	8. police officer	13. barber	18. bank
4. pharmacy	9. fire station	14. superintendent	19. school
5. sidewalk	10. post office	15. plumber	20. library

_____

_____

_____

_____

_____

_____

_____

_____

_____

_____

_____

_____

_____

_____

_____

_____

_____

_____

Unit 9
Restaurant Words

waitress

napkin

counter

ladies' room

salad

booth

order

entrance

pasta

espresso

sandwich

men's room

dessert

check

appetizer

reservation

table

menu

takeout

waiter

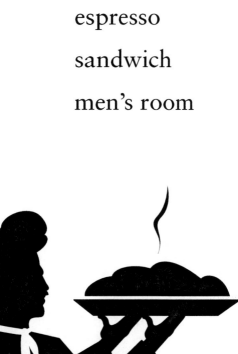

New Words and Lost Letters

Read each word and its definition. In the Lost Letters column, write each word by filling in the missing letters.

LOST LETTERS

1. booth — a partly enclosed space with a table and seats for several people — b _ _ h

2. counter — a long table — c _ _ nt _ _

3. menu — a list of food served in a restaurant — me _ _

4. order — a serving of food asked for in a restaurant — or _ _ _

5. napkin — a folded cloth or paper used at meals for protecting clothing and for wiping lips or fingers — n _ _ k _ _

6. ladies' room — a bathroom for women and girls — l _ _ i _ _ r _ _ m

7. men's room — a bathroom for men and boys — me _ _ _ oo _

8. pasta — a dish of cooked macaroni, spaghetti, or such — p _ _ t _

9. reservation — an arrangement to have a table ready for a person — _ _ se _ _ a _ i _ n

10. appetizer — food eaten before a meal to increase the desire for more food — a _ _ e _ ize _

11. salad — a dish of raw vegetables — sal _ _

12. sandwich — slices of bread with a filling between them — _ and _ i _ _

13. dessert — food eaten at the end of a meal — d _ _ _ e _ t

14. takeout — food removed from a restaurant and eaten somewhere else — t _ _ e _ _ t

15. waitress — a woman who serves food — w _ _ t _ _ _ s

16. waiter — a man who serves food — wai _ _ _

17. table — a piece of furniture having a flat top on legs — t _ _ _ _

18. espresso — coffee brewed by forcing steam through dark roasted beans — e _ p _ e _ _ o

19. check — a written statement of the amount owed in a restaurant — c _ _ _ k

20. entrance — a place through which a person goes in or comes in — _ ntr _ _ _ _

Snoop and Solve

Find the words in the maze and circle them. The words may go across, up, down, or diagonally. Check them off in the list at the top as you find them.

___ 1. booth

___ 2. counter

___ 3. menu

___ 4. order

___ 5. napkin

___ 6. ladies' room

___ 7. men's room

___ 8. pasta

___ 9. reservation

___ 10. appetizer

___ 11. salad

___ 12. sandwich

___ 13. dessert

___ 14. takeout

___ 15. waitress

___ 16. waiter

___ 17. table

___ 18. espresso

___ 19. check

___ 20. entrance

m	e	n	u	n	c	h	e	c	k	m	e	c	n
e	e	i	k	o	a	o	g	n	i	j	v	o	a
n	o	n	p	w	a	r	n	k	m	o	i	u	p
s	s	s	a	l	a	d	u	o	n	t	e	n	k
r	s	r	s	b	p	e	o	p	a	a	l	t	i
o	e	h	t	a	o	r	l	v	p	k	b	e	n
o	r	c	a	t	s	o	r	a	p	e	a	r	e
m	p	i	h	e	r	e	t	n	e	o	t	l	c
e	s	w	i	h	s	a	k	h	t	u	r	c	n
m	e	d	g	e	l	o	y	o	i	t	e	u	a
u	a	n	r	c	c	h	e	c	z	r	s	n	r
l	v	a	t	w	a	i	t	r	e	s	s	n	t
o	m	s	s	w	a	i	t	e	r	o	e	e	n
r	e	s	e	r	v	a	t	i	o	n	d	m	e

Scrambled Eggs

Write the words correctly.   **Divide the words into syllables.**

1. othob   _____   _____

2. ounertc   _____   _____

3. unme   _____   _____

4. derro   _____   _____

5. ainkpn   _____   _____

6. l'ieads romo   _____   _____

7. n'sem moro   _____   _____

8. satap   _____   _____

9. vationserre   _____   _____

10. ppetzeria   _____   _____

11. adlsa   _____   _____

12. chdanwis   _____   _____

13. sseertd   _____   _____

14. keatout   _____   _____

15. resswait   _____   _____

16. aiertw   _____   _____

17. aeblt   _____   _____

18. seepross   _____   _____

19. kechc   _____   _____

20. trenneca   _____   _____

          Survival Vocabulary

Pick a Pair

Write the number of each definition in front of the word it goes with.

____ booth

____ counter

____ menu

____ order

____ napkin

____ ladies' room

____ men's room

____ pasta

____ reservation

____ appetizer

____ salad

____ sandwich

____ dessert

____ takeout

____ waitress

____ waiter

____ table

____ espresso

____ check

____ entrance

1. food eaten at the end of a meal

2. a place through which a person goes in or comes in

3. a dish of cooked macaroni, spaghetti, or such

4. coffee brewed by forcing steam through dark roasted beans

5. a partly enclosed space with a table and seats for several people

6. a list of food served in a restaurant

7. a written statement of the amount owed in a restaurant

8. slices of bread with a filling between them

9. a dish of raw vegetables

10. food removed from a restaurant and eaten somewhere else

11. a man who serves food

12. a bathroom for men and boys

13. a piece of furniture having a flat top on legs

14. food eaten before a meal to increase the desire for more food

15. a woman who serves food

16. a bathroom for women and girls

17. a serving of food asked for in a restaurant

18. a long table

19. an arrangement to have a table ready for a person

20. a folded cloth or paper used at meals for protecting clothing and for wiping lips or fingers

Crack the Code

1 - a	6 - f	11 - k	16 - p	21 - u	24 - x
2 - b	7 - g	12 - l	17 - q	22 - v	25 - y
3 - c	8 - h	13 - m	18 - r	23 - w	26 - z
4 - d	9 - i	14 - n	19 - s		
5 - e	10 - j	15 - o	20 - t		

Write the letters under the numbers below to crack the code.

9 - 13 - 1 - 4 - 5 - 1 - 18 - 5 - 19 - 5 - 18 - 22 - 1 - 20 - 9 - 15 - 14.

20 - 8 - 1 - 20 - 2 - 15 - 15 - 20 - 8 - 9 - 19 - 5 - 13 - 16 - 20 - 25.

20 - 8 - 5 - 23 - 1 - 9 - 20 - 18 - 5 - 19 - 19 - 8 - 1 - 19 - 15 - 21 - 18 - 15 - 18 - 4 - 5 - 18.

9 - 12 - 15 - 22 - 5 - 4 - 5 - 19 - 19 - 5 - 18 - 20.

9 - 19 - 15 - 21 - 18 - 3 - 8 - 5 - 3 - 11 - 18 - 5 - 1 - 4 - 25 - 25 - 5 - 20.

20 - 8 - 5 - 20 - 1 - 2 - 12 - 5 - 9 - 19 - 14 - 5 - 1 - 18 - 20 - 8 - 5 - 5 - 14 - 20 - 18 - 1 -

14 - 3 - 5.

Write your own coded message here. Ask your partner to crack it.

Name _____

Date _____

UNIT 9: RESTAURANT WORDS

Sentence Sense

Read each sentence. One of the three sentences sounds correct. Circle the letter in front of the correct sentence.

1. (a) I dropped my booth on the floor.
   (b) We can sit in that big booth on the right.
   (c) Hand the cashier the booth so we may pay the bill.

2. (a) Let's sit at the counter and have our lunch.
   (b) I'm going to the counter to wash my hands.
   (c) Please order me a counter when the waitress comes.

3. (a) Please help me menu this chair next to the table.
   (b) The menu in this dish is too hot to eat.
   (c) The waiter gave me the menu to look at to choose my food.

4. (a) She's waiting to take our order for supper.
   (b) She likes to sit at the same order every day.
   (c) Let's all sit in the order by the window.

5. (a) My napkin tastes delicious.
   (b) Please hand me a napkin for my lap.
   (c) He always orders napkin for his lunch.

6. (a) The ladies' room is the first door on the left of the hallway.
   (b) Our ladies' room will take our order for food when she comes.
   (c) The boys should use the ladies' room.

7. (a) The men may wash in the men's room.
   (b) Ask the girls to use the men's room before we leave.
   (c) Our men's room is at our table to take our food order.

8. (a) Please tell me what pasta is available on the menu.
   (b) She'll bring all of our food on a large pasta.
   (c) Our pasta left at eight o'clock.

9. (a) Please make our dinner reservation for six o'clock tonight.
   (b) The reservation tells us how much we need to pay for the food.
   (c) The reservation shows a list of food we may order.

(continued)

© 1981, 1996 J. Weston Walch, Publisher

Survival Vocabulary

Sentence Sense *(continued)*

10. (a) The chicken soup is a good appetizer.
    (b) The appetizer in the corner is large enough for us to sit in.
    (c) This appetizer will take our order when we're ready.

11. (a) That salad will bring us our food when it's ready.
    (b) We must pay the salad before we leave the restaurant.
    (c) This salad is made of fresh vegetables.

12. (a) This big sandwich tastes so good.
    (b) He takes a long time to read the sandwich before he decides.
    (c) Let's sit in the sandwich until our table is ready.

13. (a) We always eat dessert at the end of the meal.
    (b) Let's pay the dessert before we leave the restaurant.
    (c) We can sit at this dessert to eat our lunch.

14. (a) This takeout order was cooked just the way I like it.
    (b) This takeout will take our order when we're ready.
    (c) Our takeout at that hall is for tomorrow.

15. (a) That man is the waitress for all of these tables.
    (b) We can sit in the waitress while our table is cleared.
    (c) The woman in the black and white dress is our waitress.

16. (a) That waiter took our order a few minutes ago.
    (b) She's a very tall waiter.
    (c) I'm going to the waiter to wash my hands.

17. (a) I can't read the table because it's too dark in here.
    (b) This table is large enough to hold all our food.
    (c) I'll pay the table for everyone's dinner.

18. (a) I'd like to wait in the espresso until our table is ready.
    (b) We can give our food espresso to that waiter now.
    (c) This espresso tastes delicious with dessert.

19. (a) That man who takes the money is the check in this restaurant.
    (b) We can sit at the check to eat our supper tonight.
    (c) The check tells us how much we need to pay the cashier.

20. (a) My mother will pay the entrance for our lunch.
    (b) Let's sit in that booth near the entrance.
    (c) We can give our food order to the entrance now.

   Survival Vocabulary

Pen the Pig

1. Divide the list of words in Exercise 1 into two lists of ten words each.
2. Choose a partner. Give your partner one of the lists of ten words. You keep the other list.
3. Say one of the words on your list. Your partner writes it down on a sheet of paper.
4. You check your partner's spelling.
5. If the word is spelled correctly, your partner may touch his or her pencil to a dot and draw one straight line across or down to another dot.
6. If the word is not spelled correctly, your partner may not draw a line.
7. Now your partner says one of the words on his or her list to you. You write it down.
8. Your partner checks the spelling.
9. If the word is spelled correctly, you may draw one line between two dots, going across or down.
10. If the word is not spelled correctly, you may not draw a line.
11. You and your partner take turns saying and writing words. Say a new word on the list each time.
12. Each time you draw a line, you are building a pen for the pig.
13. The object of this game is to be the person to draw the **last** line to make a square. This square is one pen. Put your initials in that pen. That pen is yours.
14. Watch the lines. Try to be the **last** person to draw the line to make a square.
15. When you and your partner have each written ten words, switch lists. Take turns saying and writing words again. Decide how many times you want to switch lists.
16. When you have finished switching lists, or when there are no more dots to use, the game is over.
17. Count the number of squares holding your initials.
18. The person with the most pens wins.

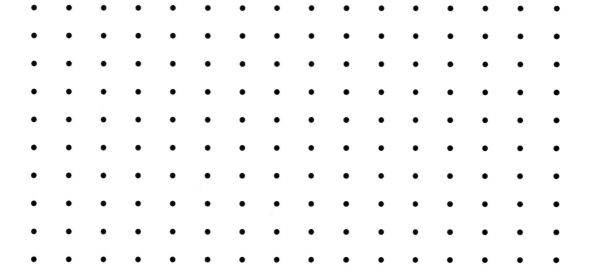

Backward Puzzle

Write a brief definition or clue for each word in the puzzle.

1.		a	p	p	e	t	i	z	e	r
2.				n	a	p	k	i	n	
3.		b	o	o	t	h				
4.	t	a	k	e	o	u	t			
5.			c	o	u	n	t	e	r	
6.		w	a	i	t	e	r			
7.			t	a	b	l	e			
8.		m	e	n	u					
9.		o	r	d	e	r				
10.		e	n	t	r	a	n	c	e	
11.	r	e	s	e	r	v	a	t	i	o	n
			y							
12.		m	e	n	s	r	o	o	m	
13.	l	a	d	i	e	s	r	o	o	m
14.	s	a	n	d	w	i	c	h		
15.		p	a	s	t	a				
16.			s	a	l	a	d			
17.			e	s	p	r	e	s	s	o
18.		w	a	i	t	r	e	s	s	
19.			c	h	e	c	k			
20.		d	e	s	s	e	r	t		

1. _____

2. _____

3. _____

4. _____

5. _____

6. _____

7. _____

8. _____

9. _____

10. _____

11. _____

12. _____

13. _____

14. _____

15. _____

16. _____

17. _____

18. _____

19. _____

20. _____

Find the hidden sentence that reads from the top down in the puzzle.
Write it here.

_____

         Survival Vocabulary

Sneaky Snakes

Dissect (cut apart) these snakes by drawing lines through their bodies after every word. Write your starting, finishing, and total times for each snake. Try to do each snake faster than the last one.

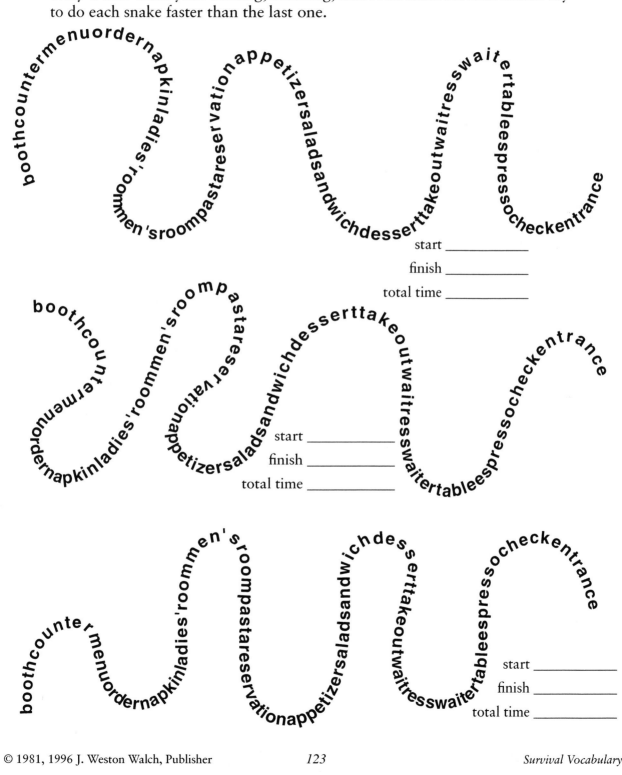

start _____

finish _____

total time _____

start _____

finish _____

total time _____

start _____

finish _____

total time _____

Name _____

Date _____

X-ray Vision

Write each word correctly.   **Write the words in alphabetical order.**

1. bueth   _____   _____

2. cowntur   _____   _____

3. menyou   _____   _____

4. ordur   _____   _____

5. naapken   _____   _____

6. laydees ruem   _____   _____

7. menz ruem   _____   _____

8. postah   _____   _____

9. rezurvashun   _____   _____

10. appatizur   _____   _____

11. saled   _____   _____

12. saandwitch   _____   _____

13. deezurt   _____   _____

14. taakowt   _____   _____

15. waaytruzz   _____   _____

16. waaytur   _____   _____

17. taybul   _____   _____

18. expresto   _____   _____

19. chek   _____   _____

20. ntruns   _____   _____

124   *Survival Vocabulary*

Silly Dilly

Write a story using all of the following words. Make it interesting!

1. booth	6. ladies' room	11. salad	16. waiter
2. counter	7. men's room	12. sandwich	17. table
3. menu	8. pasta	13. dessert	18. espresso
4. order	9. reservation	14. takeout	19. check
5. napkin	10. appetizer	15. waitress	20. entrance

_____

_____

_____

_____

_____

_____

_____

_____

_____

_____

_____

_____

_____

_____

_____

_____

_____

 Survival Vocabulary

Unit 10
Travel Words

ticket	train	seat belt
motorcycle	subway	fare
truck	helmet	elevator
driver	bicycle	pilot
airplane		conductor
bus		cab
car		boat
walk		map

Survival Vocabulary

New Words and Lost Letters

Read each word and its definition. In the Lost Letters column, write each word by filling in the missing letters.

LOST LETTERS

1. bus — a large motor vehicle that can carry many people and usually follows a regular route — _ _ s

2. train — a line of connected railroad cars on a track, pulled or pushed by a locomotive — _ _ _ in

3. cab — a car for public use with a driver who is paid — c _ _

4. car — a four-wheeled motor vehicle driven on streets — _ _ r

5. airplane — a machine with wings that flies in the air — _ _ _ pl _ _ _

6. subway — an underground electric railway — s _ _ w _ _

7. boat — a watercraft moved by oars, sails, or engine — _ _ _ t

8. bicycle — a vehicle to ride on with two wheels, handlebars, a seat, and foot pedals to move it — _ _ c _ cl _

9. truck — a vehicle for hauling loads along the streets — _ _ _ _ k

10. ticket — a small printed card that gives a person a specific right — _ _ c _ _ _

11. conductor — a person in charge of passengers who collects fares — co _ _ _ c _ _ _

12. driver — a person who makes a vehicle move — d _ _ _ er

13. walk — to move along on foot — _ _ l _

14. pilot — a person who flies an airplane or steers a boat — p _ _ o _

15. elevator — a small cage-like room that moves people from floor to floor in tall buildings — _ _ _ v _ t _ _

16. helmet — a protective covering for the head — _ _ l _ _ t

17. seat belt — a strap that holds a person in a seat — _ e _ t _ el _

18. fare — the amount of money paid for a ride — _ a _ _

19. motorcycle — a two-wheeled vehicle moved by an engine, larger and heavier than a bicycle — _ _ _ _ _ cycle

20. map — a chart that shows roads, cities, and other surface features — _ _ p

Survival Vocabulary

Snoop and Solve

Find the words in the maze and circle them. The words may go across, up, down, or diagonally. Check them off in the list at the top as you find them.

___ 1. bus   ___ 8. bicycle   ___ 15. elevator

___ 2. train   ___ 9. truck   ___ 16. helmet

___ 3. cab   ___ 10. ticket   ___ 17. seat belt

___ 4. car   ___ 11. conductor   ___ 18. fare

___ 5. airplane   ___ 12. driver   ___ 19. motorcycle

___ 6. subway   ___ 13. walk   ___ 20. map

___ 7. boat   ___ 14. pilot

s	e	b	m	s	e	a	t	b	e	l	t	e	t
o	s	o	o	a	b	r	c	r	t	t	r	o	o
s	e	a	t	o	p	i	o	i	e	r	t	a	l
b	f	t	o	e	o	e	n	v	w	u	a	e	i
i	o	e	r	b	l	a	d	d	a	c	f	i	p
c	e	a	c	c	t	a	u	o	r	k	a	e	n
y	f	t	y	a	r	e	c	o	d	i	g	r	t
c	t	c	c	t	c	n	t	r	e	a	v	e	t
l	i	a	l	n	t	a	o	c	s	b	m	e	e
b	r	o	e	t	v	l	r	o	s	l	k	o	r
k	m	k	o	e	i	p	o	n	e	c	n	f	e
l	o	n	l	c	c	r	r	h	i	e	b	a	c
a	e	e	f	a	k	i	g	t	g	d	n	u	o
w	r	s	u	b	w	a	y	a	u	c	t	r	s

ROAD MAP

Survival Vocabulary

Scrambled Eggs

Write the words correctly.   **Divide the words into syllables.**

1. sub _____ _____

2. airnt _____ _____

3. abc _____ _____

4. rac _____ _____

5. neplraia _____ _____

6. waybsu _____ _____

7. toab _____ _____

8. cycelbi _____ _____

9. uckrt _____ _____

10. ckteit _____ _____

11. ducrotnoc _____ _____

12. verird _____ _____

13. lawk _____ _____

14. ploit _____ _____

15. toreelva _____ _____

16. thelem _____ _____

17. east telb _____ _____

18. erfa _____ _____

19. cclyemootr _____ _____

20. apm _____ _____

Survival Vocabulary

Name _____

Date _____

Pick a Pair

Write the number of each definition in front of the word it goes with.

____ bus   1. an underground electric railway

____ train   2. a person who makes a vehicle move

____ cab   3. a vehicle for hauling loads along the streets

____ car   4. a strap that holds a person in a seat

____ airplane   5. the amount of money paid for a ride

____ subway   6. a small printed card that gives a person a specific right

____ boat   7. a line of connected railroad cars on a track, pulled or pushed by a locomotive

____ bicycle   8. a chart that shows roads, cities, and other surface features

____ truck   9. a person who flies an airplane or steers a boat

____ ticket   10. a two-wheeled vehicle moved by an engine, larger and heavier than a bicycle

____ conductor   11. a protective covering for the head

____ driver   12. a large motor vehicle that can carry many people and usually follows a regular route

____ walk   13. to move along on foot

____ pilot   14. a car for public use with a driver who is paid

____ elevator   15. a four-wheeled motor-driven vehicle on streets

____ helmet   16. a machine with wings that flies in the air

____ seat belt   17. a small cage-like room that moves people from floor to floor in tall buildings

____ fare   18. a person in change of passengers who collects fares

____ motorcycle   19. a watercraft moved by oars, sails, or engine

____ map   20. a vehicle to ride on with two wheels, handlebars, a seat, and foot pedals to move it

    131   *Survival Vocabulary*

Crack the Code

1 - a	6 - f	11 - k	16 - p	21 - u	24 - x
2 - b	7 - g	12 - l	17 - q	22 - v	25 - y
3 - c	8 - h	13 - m	18 - r	23 - w	26 - z
4 - d	9 - i	14 - n	19 - s		
5 - e	10 - j	15 - o	20 - t		

Write the letters under the numbers below to crack the code.

20 - 8 - 5 - 3 - 15 - 14 - 4 - 21 - 3 - 20 - 15 - 18 - 23 - 1 - 22 - 5 - 4 - 20 - 15 - 21 - 19 - 6 - 18 -

15 - 13 - 20 - 8 - 5 - 20 - 18 - 1 - 9 - 14.

20 - 8 - 1 - 20 - 13 - 15 - 20 - 15 - 18 - 3 - 25 - 3 - 12 - 5 - 2 - 5 - 12 - 15 - 14 - 7 - 19 - 20 - 15 -

13 - 5.

9 - 16 - 1 - 9 - 4 - 13 - 25 - 6 - 1 - 18 - 5 - 20 - 15 - 18 - 9 - 4 - 5 - 15 - 14 - 20 - 8 - 5 - 2 - 21 - 19.

20 - 8 - 1 - 20 - 1 - 9 - 18 - 16 - 12 - 1 - 14 - 5 - 3 - 1 - 18 - 18 - 9 - 5 - 19 - 13 - 1 - 14 - 25 -

16 - 5 - 15 - 16 - 12 - 5.

9 - 18 - 9 - 4 - 5 - 15 - 14 - 20 - 8 - 5 - 19 - 21 - 2 - 23 - 1 - 25 - 5 - 22 - 5 - 18 - 25 - 4 - 1 - 25 -

15 - 6 - 20 - 8 - 5 - 23 - 5 - 5 - 11.

20 - 8 - 5 - 5 - 12 - 5 - 22 - 1 - 20 - 15 - 18 - 23 - 9 - 12 - 12 - 20 - 1 - 11 - 5 - 21 - 19 - 21 - 16.

On the back of this page, write your own coded message. Ask your partner to
crack it.

                   Survival Vocabulary

Sentence Sense

Read each sentence. One of the three sentences sounds correct. Circle the letter in front of the correct sentence.

1. (a) We can all ride the bus to the next town.
   (b) Let's bus up this elevator to the next floor.
   (c) When we get on this ride, we'll hand the man a bus as our fare.

2. (a) Please buy my train as my fare to ride this bus.
   (b) This train has four rubber wheels on it to carry all of us.
   (c) This train has many windows through which we can see the country.

3. (a) That yellow cab goes up and down in tall buildings.
   (b) That yellow cab is a car which will take us to the city.
   (c) This cab can fly over the river.

4. (a) My older brother just bought a car for our family.
   (b) Please help me read the car to find the correct street.
   (c) My father's car rides on a track and carries over fifty people.

5. (a) This airplane carries people to many places under the ground.
   (b) We all came to this country in a very big airplane.
   (c) An airplane only moves around on the ground.

6. (a) I love to go from street to street underground on the subway.
   (b) We can park our little subway between those two cars.
   (c) Please buy two subways from the conductor.

7. (a) That boat travels from town to town on a long track.
   (b) That big boat is floating in the ocean.
   (c) Please help me read the boat to see where we are.

8. (a) My uncle bought us a new bicycle for a holiday present.
   (b) His family flew to this country on a shiny bicycle.
   (c) My mother paid the bicycle for our family to ride the bus.

9. (a) Let's load up that big truck with all of our furniture.
   (b) That big truck will take off into the sky in a moment.
   (c) She rode the truck up to the sixth floor in that building.

(continued)

Survival Vocabulary

Sentence Sense *(continued)*

10. (a) He forgot to buy a ticket for me to ride on the train.
    (b) Please stand and let that old man sit in your ticket.
    (c) That ticket is so loud when the motor starts.

11. (a) He can't park the conductor in that parking space.
    (b) This airplane has two women conductors.
    (c) The man who takes the tickets on this train is the conductor.

12. (a) The driver of that car is a good friend of my dad's.
    (b) Please buy five drivers so that we can all ride the bus.
    (c) The driver to ride to the next town is fifty cents.

13. (a) My sister has a walk for us to go to the shopping mall.
    (b) They are reading the signs to see which way to go on their walk.
    (c) My mother called the driver to help us find a walk to travel.

14. (a) Please tell the pilot on that bus to help us find a seat.
    (b) The pilot on our airplane said we were landing.
    (c) My sister asked the pilot which street we stopped at.

15. (a) I love to ride the elevator up and down in our building.
    (b) He tried to park the elevator between those two cars.
    (c) Please hand the conductor my elevator.

16. (a) I bought a helmet to wear when riding my bicycle.
    (b) Many people can ride on that helmet to the city.
    (c) My aunt loves to helmet on the train to come to visit us.

17. (a) The voice on our seat belt was kind and helpful.
    (b) Fasten your seat belt before getting underway.
    (c) That seat belt is going to hit that car because it's speeding.

18. (a) The fare to ride from here to Main Street is twenty-five cents.
    (b) My grandfather bought me a new fare for my birthday.
    (c) Please call the fare to make reservations on that flight.

19. (a) Our motorcycle has many cars being pulled on a long track.
    (b) That motorcycle is loud when the motor is running.
    (c) At least fifty people can ride in that motorcycle.

20. (a) If we read this map correctly, we won't get lost traveling.
    (b) That map travels underground at a very fast rate.
    (c) Please ask the map how soon we'll get to the city.

 Survival Vocabulary

Pen the Pig

1. Divide the list of words in Exercise 1 into two lists of ten words each.
2. Choose a partner. Give your partner one of the lists of ten words. You keep the other list.
3. Say one of the words on your list. Your partner writes it down on a sheet of paper.
4. You check your partner's spelling.
5. If the word is spelled correctly, your partner may touch his or her pencil to a dot and draw one straight line across or down to another dot.
6. If the word is not spelled correctly, your partner may not draw a line.
7. Now your partner says one of the words on his or her list to you. You write it down.
8. Your partner checks the spelling.
9. If the word is spelled correctly, you may draw one line between two dots, going across or down.
10. If the word is not spelled correctly, you may not draw a line.
11. You and your partner take turns saying and writing words. Say a new word on the list each time.
12. Each time you draw a line, you are building a pen for the pig.
13. The object of this game is to be the person to draw the **last** line to make a square. This square is one pen. Put your initials in that pen. That pen is yours.
14. Watch the lines. Try to be the **last** person to draw the line to make a square.
15. When you and your partner have each written ten words, switch lists. Take turns saying and writing words again. Decide how many times you want to switch lists.
16. When you have finished switching lists, or when there are no more dots to use, the game is over.
17. Count the number of squares holding your initials.
18. The person with the most pens wins.

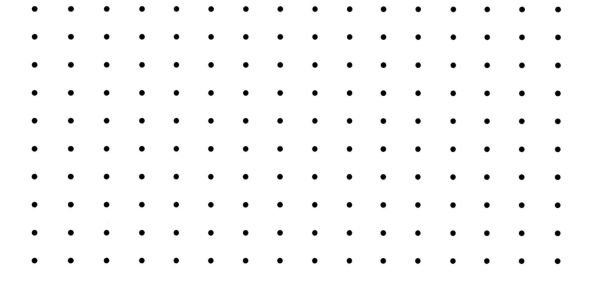

Name _____

Date _____

Backward Puzzle

Write a brief definition or clue for each word in the puzzle.

1.		w	a	l	k					
2.			b	o	a	t				
3.		p	i	l	o	t				
4.		t	i	c	k	e	t			
5.				f	a	r	e			
6.		m	o	t	o	r	c	y	c	l	e
7.			c	a	r					
8.		a	i	r	p	l	a	n	e	
9.			h	e	l	m	e	t		
10.			m	a	p					
11.			c	a	b					
12.		e	l	e	v	a	t	o	r	
13.			s	u	b	w	a	y		
14.			t	r	u	c	k			
15.			c	o	n	d	u	c	t	o	r
16.		d	r	i	v	e	r			
17.		t	r	a	i	n				
18.		b	u	s						
19.			b	i	c	y	c	l	e	
20.		s	e	a	t	b	e	l	t	

1. _____
2. _____
3. _____
4. _____
5. _____
6. _____
7. _____
8. _____
9. _____
10. _____
11. _____
12. _____
13. _____
14. _____
15. _____
16. _____
17. _____
18. _____
19. _____
20. _____

Find the hidden sentence that reads from the top down in the puzzle.
Write it here.

_____

Survival Vocabulary

Sneaky Snakes

Dissect (cut apart) these snakes by drawing lines through their bodies after every word. Write your starting, finishing, and total times for each snake. Try to do each snake faster than the last one.

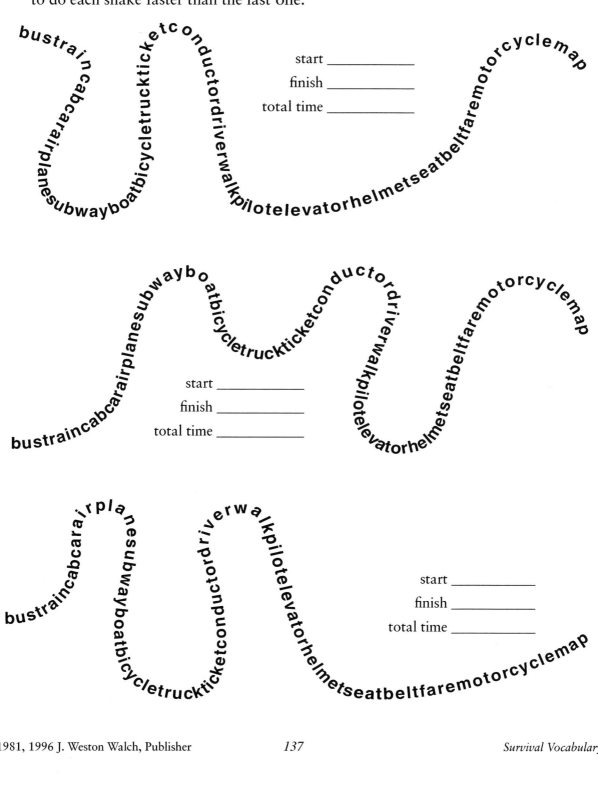

start _____

finish _____

total time _____

start _____

finish _____

total time _____

start _____

finish _____

total time _____

X-ray Vision

Write each word correctly.   **Write the words in alphabetical order.**

1. buuss _____   _____

2. traaynn _____   _____

3. cahbb _____   _____

4. cahur _____   _____

5. ayerplaann _____   _____

6. ssubwaay _____   _____

7. boout _____   _____

8. bisiicul _____   _____

9. truk _____   _____

10. tikit _____   _____

11. conduktur _____   _____

12. dryvur _____   _____

13. wock _____   _____

14. pylett _____   _____

15. ellihvaaturr _____   _____

16. hellmut _____   _____

17. seeet bellet _____   _____

18. fayur _____   _____

19. motursikul _____   _____

20. mahhpp _____   _____

Silly Dilly

Write a story using all of the following words. Make it interesting!

1. bus
2. train
3. cab
4. car
5. airplane

6. subway
7. boat
8. bicycle
9. truck
10. ticket

11. conductor
12. driver
13. walk
14. pilot
15. elevator

16. helmet
17. seat belt
18. fare
19. motorcycle
20. map

_____

_____

_____

_____

_____

_____

_____

_____

_____

_____

_____

_____

_____

_____

_____

_____

_____

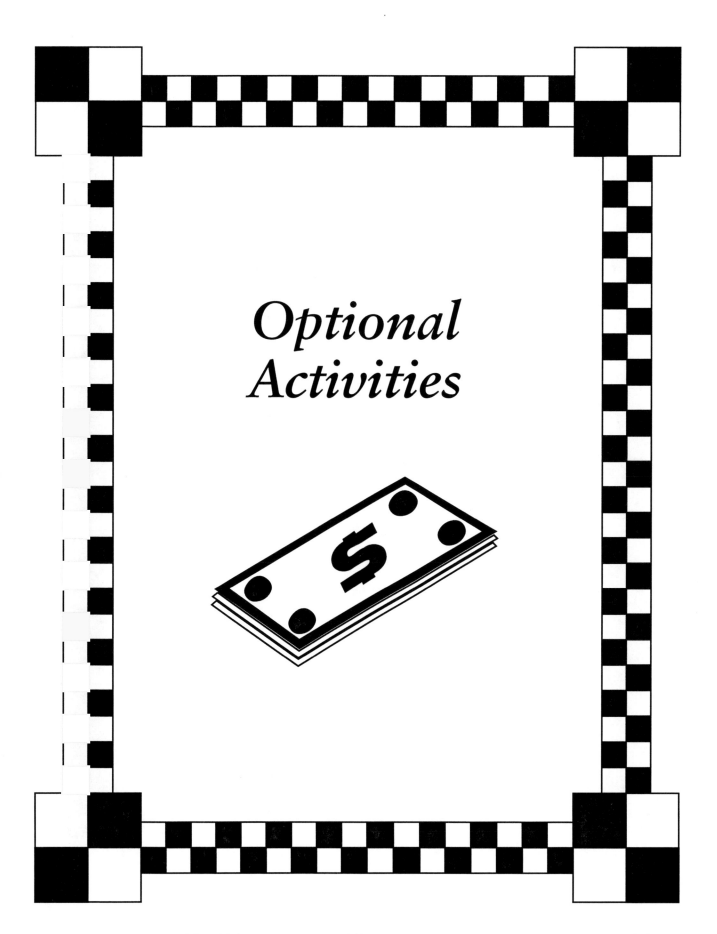

Optional Activities

Word Bankbook

Cut on the cutting line. Fold on the folding line. You now have a bankbook. Draw your own front cover on this book. Each time the banker stamps one of your Word Bank Checks, the banker will write the amount of the check in this book in a column marked *deposits*. Each time your earnings total $1000.00, you will receive a Preferred Customer Sticker from the banker. Glue the sticker in the book. Show it to your teacher. The sticker entitles you to a classroom privilege named by your teacher.

CUT

deposits

deposits

deposits

deposits

FOLD

deposits

deposits

deposits

deposits

Brain Teaser

1. Write as many new words on the lines below as you can remember from the unit you have just studied.
2. Your partner will check your spelling. You earn $10.00 in Word Money for each word spelled correctly.
3. Your partner will dictate the rest of the words from the unit. You earn $5.00 in Word Money for each dictated word you spell correctly.
4. You receive no money for wrong words.
5. Your partner adds up your earnings.
6. Your partner writes out a check for the total amount and gives the check to you.
7. You sign the check on the back and give it to your partner with your Word Bankbook. Your partner will deposit this amount in your Word Bankbook.
8. Write any missed words ten times on the Study Sheets. Study them.
9. Ask your partner to test you on these words another time for credit in your Word Bankbook; you earn $5.00 in Word Money for each word spelled correctly.
10. When your Word Bankbook shows total earnings of $1000.00, your partner will give you a Preferred Customer Sticker. Glue it in your Bankbook. Show it to your teacher and you will get a classroom privilege.
11. Now try to earn another $1000.00, and another Preferred Customer Sticker, by studying your new list of words from the next unit.

		Word Money Earned			Word Money Earned
1.	_____	_____	11.	_____	_____
2.	_____	_____	12.	_____	_____
3.	_____	_____	13.	_____	_____
4.	_____	_____	14.	_____	_____
5.	_____	_____	15.	_____	_____
6.	_____	_____	16.	_____	_____
7.	_____	_____	17.	_____	_____
8.	_____	_____	18.	_____	_____
9.	_____	_____	19.	_____	_____
10.	_____	_____	20.	_____	_____

total _____   total _____

_____ total—first column

and _____ total—second column

_____ total for deposit in Bankbook

Monthly Moneymaker

Write as many words as you can remember from the units you have studied. Your partner will check them and give you $10.00 in Word Money for each word spelled correctly. Write the rest of the words from dictation. Check your own spelling. You earn $5.00 in Word Money for each word spelled correctly. Add 5% to your total earnings for this test. Deposit this total in your Word Bankbook.

	Word Money Earned		**Word Money Earned**
_____	_____	_____	_____
_____	_____	_____	_____
_____	_____	_____	_____
_____	_____	_____	_____
_____	_____	_____	_____
_____	_____	_____	_____
_____	_____	_____	_____
_____	_____	_____	_____
_____	_____	_____	_____
_____	_____	_____	_____
_____	_____	_____	_____
_____	_____	_____	_____
_____	_____	_____	_____
_____	_____	_____	_____
_____	_____	_____	_____

total _____

plus 5% of total _____

total for deposit in Bankbook _____

Name _____

Date _____

Study Sheets

Write each word at least ten times that you missed on a Brain Teaser or
Monthly Moneymaker. Say each letter as you write it. When you are sure you
know the word, put your pencil on the next line, close your eyes, and write the
word. Try to see the word in your mind. Good luck! When you know these
words, ask your partner to retest you on them. Add your earnings to your
Word Bankbook.

_____   _____   _____

_____   _____   _____

_____   _____   _____

_____   _____   _____

_____   _____   _____

_____   _____   _____

_____   _____   _____

_____   _____   _____

_____   _____   _____

_____   _____   _____

_____   _____   _____

_____   _____   _____

_____   _____   _____

_____   _____   _____

_____   _____   _____

Word Bank Checks

Your partner makes out one of these banking checks for the Word Money you've earned. You sign it on the back, and deposit it in your Word Bankbook by giving it back to the banker. After the banker has written the deposit in your Bankbook, you will get the check back. Keep these checks in an envelope or workbook pocket as proof of your earnings.

Word Bank Check

19 _____

PAY TO THE
ORDER OF _____

$ _____

_____ DOLLARS

Word Bank Check

Word Bank Check

19 _____

PAY TO THE
ORDER OF _____

$ _____

_____ DOLLARS

Word Bank Check

Word Bank Check

19 _____

PAY TO THE
ORDER OF _____

$ _____

_____ DOLLARS

Word Bank Check

Flash Cards

Cut out these cards and write a vocabulary word on each one. Keep them in an envelope or notebook pocket for practice.

Survival Vocabulary